RIGHT BEFORE OUR EYES

REVEALING THE TIMES WE ARE IN

TRILOGY
A WHOLLY OWNED SUBSIDIARY OF TBN
PROFESSIONAL PUBLISHING MEETS POWERFUL PROMOTION

TRILOGY
A WHOLLY OWNED SUBSIDIARY OF **TBN**
PROFESSIONAL PUBLISHING MEETS POWERFUL PROMOTION

Trilogy Christian Publishers
A Wholly Owned Subsidiary of Trinity Broadcasting Network
2442 Michelle Drive
Tustin, CA 92780
Copyright © 2025 by Jonathan Frohms
Scripture quotations marked NIV are taken from the Holy Bible, New International Version®, NIV®. Copyright © 1973, 1978, 1984, 2011 by Biblica, Inc. TM Used by permission of Zondervan. All rights reserved worldwide. www.zondervan.com. The "NIV" and "New International Version" are trademarks registered in the United States Patent and Trademark Office by Biblica, Inc.TM Scripture quotations marked NKJV are taken from the New King James Version®. Copyright © 1982 by Thomas Nelson. Used by permission. All rights reserved. Scripture quotations marked KJV are taken from the King James Version of the Bible. Public domain.
All rights reserved, including the right to reproduce this book or portions thereof in any form whatsoever.
For information, address Trilogy Christian Publishing
Rights Department, 2442 Michelle Drive, Tustin, Ca 92780.
Trilogy Christian Publishing/ TBN and colophon are trademarks of Trinity Broadcasting Network.
For information about special discounts for bulk purchases, please contact Trilogy Christian Publishing.

Trilogy Disclaimer: The views and content expressed in this book are those of the author and may not necessarily reflect the views and doctrine of Trilogy Christian Publishing or the Trinity Broadcasting Network.

10 9 8 7 6 5 4 3 2 1
Library of Congress Cataloging-in-Publication Data is available.
ISBN 979-8-89597-106-2
ISBN 979-8-89597-107-9 (ebook)

RIGHT BEFORE OUR EYES

REVEALING THE TIMES WE ARE IN

JONATHAN FROHMS

TRILOGY
A WHOLLY OWNED SUBSIDIARY OF TBN
PROFESSIONAL PUBLISHING MEETS POWERFUL PROMOTION

– DEDICATION –

To precious Mary. My wife, my love, and my greatest friend. Thank you for always standing with me and for cheering me on in running the race that God has set before me. It's a privilege living life with you!

To my parents. Thank you for raising me, loving me, and always supporting me in following God's calling on my life.

– TABLE OF CONTENTS –

Foreword	9
Preface	11
PART I: Daniel's Vision Unfolded in History	15
Chapter 1: Daniel's Vision	17
Chapter 2: The First Beast—The Lion with Eagle's Wings	23
Chapter 3: We Need Spiritual Ears	31
Chapter 4: The Second Beast—The Bear	39
Chapter 5: The Bear and the Church	49
Chapter 6: The Leopard with Four Wings and Four Heads	57
PART II: The Spirit of Antichrist and the Beasts	65
Chapter 7: The Spirit of Antichrist Among the First Beast	67
Chapter 8: The Bear and the Spirit of Antichrist	75
Chapter 9: The Legend and the Spirit of the Antichrist	99
Part III: The Fourth Beast	117
Chapter 10: Introduction into the Fourth Beast	119
Chapter 11: It Was Different from the Other Beasts	133
Chapter 12: Preparing the Way	145
Chapter 13: The Three Steps of the Antichrist	183
Chapter 14: The Small Horn	189
Chapter 15: The End-Time Bride	193
Chapter 16: John's Identical Vision	205
Chapter 17: Your Turn to Respond	215
About the Author	217

– FOREWORD –

This book is a tool that Jonathan has provided to give the body of Christ an understanding of the current and coming world situation. A condition that was foretold in the prophetic book of Daniel, written many hundreds of years ago. What you are about to read comes with a timely urgency, as it is necessary that our generation understands what lies behind us and what is ahead of us. Jonathan takes these biblical prophecies seriously and, in the same breath, uses the Word of God to explain them.

This in-depth study that Jonathan provided will not just give you information about God's plan for His church, but it will also build your faith and strengthen your stand on biblical truth.

Based on the authority of God's Word, Jonathan points out the Father's desire for us: to show His strategic ways to every believer. God never planned for us, the church, to sit on the sideline in these timely matters, but He wants us to be involved in building His kingdom through His everlasting covenant with us.

To receive from God and to feed upon His Word is not like the process at a drive-through at your favorite fast-food restaurant. You must take time to feed on it and meditate on it, then it will open up and change your life.

I pray that this timely book will be a blessing to your life. As you read this book and as you learn what God's Word has to say about the end times, remember that God has promised eternal life to every person who receives Him. As you believe in Him with all your heart, you will have no fear of the future.

—Winfried Wentland
Pastor, missionary, and technical leader with "Christ For All Nations"
Author of the book *By Life or by Death: Extreme African Exploits for the Gospel*

– PREFACE –

The centerpiece of this book is the seventh chapter of the book of Daniel. In this significant chapter, Daniel wrote down a powerful vision that he received from God. This prophetic vision unveils many details about the times that we live in. It describes four beasts that emerge before our Lord's second coming. All four beasts are different from each other, and all four beasts each have a very specific meaning. This vision also unveils critical details about the coming of the Antichrist and his characteristics. Daniel's vision speaks about seasons that I believe have already passed, current times that you and I live in and also times that are ahead of us.

It is important for all of us believers to take heed and discern in what times we are living in. We must be ready, and our hearts must be prepared for the Lord's second coming. These are not the days to be lukewarm; these are not the days to take our hands off the plow, but these are the days in which we all must follow Jesus steadfastly and wholeheartedly. In these last days, our mission as the body of Christ is not to build our own kingdom but to build His kingdom. There are too many people around us who are in despair and utter darkness. There are too many Christians who are confused and too many churches that have lost sight of what is important. There are too many Christian marriages that are falling apart, and there are too many Christian families that are broken. Too many are lacking God's power, God's truth, and God's love to overcome this fallen world. Our world is getting spiritually darker by the day, yet at the same time, sin is openly accepted like never before.

Could it be that all these things are happening because we live in the last days? Could it be that Daniel's vision speaks about these days that we are in? Could it be that Daniel's vision talks about the pressures that we are facing today? And could it be that we find answers to these problems in Daniel's vision?

My hope in writing this book is that the body of Christ would wake up, redeem the times, and prepare itself for Christ's second coming. My hope is that many would realize that the devil is cunning and that he wants to pull down as many people as possible with him into eternal damnation. We cannot afford to get eternity wrong. If we realize that we are now in the times that Daniel foresaw thousands of years ago, if we realize how close we are to the Lord's return, I believe it will give us the necessary intensity and passion to run this race. If we truly understand the urgency of His second coming, I believe a new compassion will arise in us to reach the lost. This urgency will also give us an iron focus on what is truly important in this broken and confused world.

Understanding what is happening right before our eyes gives us insight into how to build His kingdom and the necessary wisdom to stand against the powers of darkness. For every lie from the devil, there is a truth from the Father of lights. We must know these truths and speak them forth in power and authority. Truth always brings freedom, truth always brings breakthrough, and truth always penetrates the kingdom of darkness and furthers the kingdom of light. If our eyes are closed, however, how will we see the truth in the days ahead?

There are many books out there about prophecy and biblical prophecy. Some may be bang on, and some may not be. I am not writing this book to excite anyone, nor am I writing this book to captivate you. I am writing this book because I believe the Lord gave me a revelation about Daniel's vision and because I believe

He has asked me to write it. Despite my claim that the Lord gave me a revelation, we must never forget that the Bible tells us to test everything. The Bible tells us that we must judge all things by their fruit and according to scripture, so henceforth, I invite you to test this revelation and judge the fruit of it.

I say all of this because prophecy has become somewhat of a "hip" subject in the body of Christ in the last decades. People use it to stir up excitement, and unfortunately, many use it without integrity. The truth is that prophecy is not flashy; it is not "hip," nor is it shallow. Prophecy is real and solid. Prophecy is not to be given lightly but carefully, in the sensitivity of the Holy Spirit and according to the truths of scripture. Prophecy is supposed to give clear direction to the body of Christ. Prophecy encourages, but it also rebukes. It builds up, but it also tears down. It speaks forth great things, but it also warns. All that being said, I would not call this book a purely prophetic book. To me, this book is a down-to-earth Christian book that holds a lot of prophecy. This book is written for every believer, no matter what phase of life they are in. This book is for teenagers, ministers of the Gospel, seasoned Christians, and babies in Christ.

Of course I do hope that this book is very exciting to read, but just know that excitement is not the purpose—the sole aim is to open your spiritual eyes. The Holy Spirit wrote the Bible. He intended for us to know about Daniel's vision. I am confident that He intended for us to understand Daniel's vision. And He intended for us to act according to Daniel's end-time vision. So, I challenge you to read this book with an open heart and open eyes. Ask the Holy Spirit to witness to you personally about the times we are in. I pray this book will bless you and strengthen your relationship with Jesus.

PART I: DANIEL'S VISION UNFOLDED IN HISTORY

— CHAPTER 1: —
DANIEL'S VISION

THE SEVERITY OF DANIEL'S VISION

When we look at what type of man Daniel was, we discover that he was a very secure, strong man of God. At times in his life, Daniel was put under intense pressure, such as the time he was threatened with execution by King Nebuchadnezzar: He could either interpret the king's dream accurately or be killed. Now, that's what I call pressure. And, of course, we all know the famous Bible story in which Daniel was thrown into a den of hungry lions and miraculously survived. In both of these high-pressure situations, Daniel remained absolutely calm. In life, moments of pressure and danger always show the character of a person. Daniel proved that he was very strong in his faith, that he was not easily moved, and that he had no fear of death by the king's hangmen nor by fierce animals. When it comes to his vision in chapter 7, however, we see a very different reaction from Daniel. Surprisingly, we see a troubled and shaken Daniel.

"I, Daniel, was grieved in my spirit within my body, and the visions of my head troubled me" (Daniel 7:15, NKJV).

In Daniel 7:28 (NKJV), we also read, "This is the end of the account. As for me, Daniel, my thoughts greatly troubled me, and my countenance changed; but I kept the matter in my heart."

Notice that Daniel states twice how greatly troubled he was by this end-time vision. Through all of it, it was specifically the fourth beast that affected him. In Daniel 7:19 (NKJV), Daniel said, "Then I wished to know the truth about the fourth beast, which was… exceedingly dreadful."

Daniel did not waver in his faith after receiving this vision, nor do I believe that there was any fear of death in him, but it is clear to see that this vision shook Daniel to the core. If a secure man like Daniel was troubled by what he saw, we must realize how important it is for us to understand this vision. After all, we are living in Daniel's future, and we are living in a world that looks, in many ways, just like his vision. Just like Daniel, we must ask God for an interpretation. My question to you is the following: Does the church realize the importance and severity of this vision? Could it be that we are living in those last days that this vision describes?

The truth is that this vision that shook Daniel to the core has been unfolding over the last few thousand years, and any day, the rule of the Antichrist could begin. Since Daniel died, Jesus has come, Jesus has died for us, Jesus has risen and has returned to heaven. He is coming back soon, and we must heed this vision that Daniel received from God. It was not given by accident, but I believe that it is in the Bible and that it is for us so that we can be prepared for what is coming.

SOME BASIC INFORMATION

Before we get into Daniel's vision, let us look at some basic information. We find Daniel's vision in chapter 7 of the book of Daniel. The way I see it, there are essentially four parts to Daniel's vision. When you read the seventh chapter of Daniel's vision it might help you to split his vision up into these four different parts.

Part One

Part one is about the initial vision of the four beasts. This discusses from verse one to verse eight.

Part Two

The second part of Daniel's vision is about the judgment of the four beasts and the establishing of God's eternal kingdom. This second part goes from verse nine all the way to verse fourteen.

Part Three

In the third part, Daniel receives an interpretation about the four beasts in more detail, especially in regard to the fourth beast. This part is from verse fifteen to verse twenty-two.

Part Four

The last part of this vision is, yet again, a deeper interpretation of the four beasts with even more detail. Similar to part three, the focus returns to the fourth beast. This part finishes with stating the judgment of the fourth beast and the establishing of God's eternal kingdom. This fourth part covers verse twenty-three through verse twenty-eight.

THE INITIAL VISION

In the first year of Belshazzar king of Babylon, Daniel had a dream and visions of his head while on his bed. Then he wrote down the dream, telling the main facts.

Daniel spoke, saying, "I saw in my vision by night, and behold, the four winds of heaven were stirring up the Great Sea. And four great beasts came up from the sea, each different from the other. The first was like a lion, and had eagle's wings. I watched till its wings were plucked off; and it was lifted up from the earth and made to stand on two feet like a man, and a man's heart was given to it.

"And suddenly another beast, a second, like a bear. It was raised up on one side, and had three ribs in its mouth between its teeth. And they said thus to it: 'Arise, devour much flesh!'

"After this I looked, and there was another, like a leopard, which had on its back four wings of a bird. The beast also had four heads, and dominion was given to it.

"After this I saw in the night visions, and behold, a fourth beast, dreadful and terrible, exceedingly strong. It had huge iron teeth; it was devouring, breaking in pieces, and trampling the residue with its feet. It was different from all the beasts that were before it, and it had ten horns. I was considering the horns, and there was another horn, a little one, coming up among them, before whom three of the first horns were plucked out by the roots. And there, in this horn, were eyes like the eyes of a man, and a mouth speaking pompous words."

Daniel 7:1–8 (NKJV)

I believe that each beast that is mentioned here in Daniel's vision stands for a certain era and season here on earth. A distinct period of time in which each beast has dominion and power here on earth. Each of these beasts has authority to rule this earth, and throughout its rule, it has the dominion to affect and direct humanity. We know this because, in Daniel 7:17 (NKJV), these four beasts are called kings: "Those great beasts, which are four, are four kings which arise out of the earth."

Then, in Daniel 7:23 (NKJV), the beasts are referred to as kingdoms: "The fourth beast shall be a fourth kingdom on earth, which shall be different from all other kingdoms."

To be a king means to rule over people. According to how a king rules, his kingdom and its people will be shaped. A godly king will build a godly kingdom, and an evil king will build an evil kingdom. Just like an earthly king, so do these beasts have power to rule and to shape the kingdom of this world.

It may surprise you to know that the first three beasts (the first three kings) have already appeared and stepped down from their place of dominion. We are currently living in the period of the fourth beast, the fourth king, and his kingdom is growing. Some of these four beasts' dominions have lasted longer than others, but it is important to say that all four beasts have shaped our world spiritually and naturally in very significant ways. It is not by chance that each beast in Daniel's vision appears chronologically according to how they have appeared in history. I will also go through these four beasts chronologically, just as they emerged in Daniel's vision. With that being said, let us look at the first beast: the lion with eagle's wings.

— CHAPTER 2: —
THE FIRST BEAST–THE LION WITH EAGLE'S WINGS

KINGS, LIONS, AND EAGLES

"The first was like a lion, and had eagle's wings" (Daniel 7:4, NKJV).

The first beast in Daniel's vision is the lion with eagle's wings. This beast is embodied by two animals: the lion and the eagle. The lion is a powerful animal. Even though he is not the fastest animal, not the biggest animal, not the smartest animal, and not even the strongest animal, he stands resolute as the king of the jungle and the animal kingdom. The aura around him speaks of majesty and royalty. In the African language Swahili, the word for "lion" is *simba*, and it actually means king. It is not by accident that, throughout the history of mankind, the lion has always been associated with the position of a king. Looking through history, many kings and monarchs likened themselves to lions, and many used the symbol of the lion on their banners and seals. After all, Jesus Himself identifies with the lion, and Jesus is the King of kings and Lord of lords.

Interestingly, the eagle has the same meaning as the lion. The eagle is the king of the birds and the king of the air. The eagle flies high in the skies, discerning the winds like a true leader. He is a fierce hunter, and no other bird can match his power and majestic appearance. Just like the lion, many monarchs, kings, and rulers identified themselves with the eagle. Both the lion and the eagle are sublime animals; both are rulers in their sphere, and both animals are combined in this first beast. Their attributes—royalty, power, and authority—point us straight toward the meaning of this first beast.

The lion with eagle's wings represents the age of the kings and monarchs of this world, which is, by the way, the longest era of all four beasts. This epoch started very early on in history and lasted thousands of years until the nineteenth century.

The first true form of government was the rule of kings. A better word for this type of rulership or government is the word "monarchy." Those who ruled in the era of kings that Daniel's vision describes were not always given the title of "king," but I believe that this era of kings included all rulers who demonstrated full power and authority over the people under them. The word "monarch" means "sovereign head of state." This can be an emperor, pharaoh, patriarch, or even a judge, as we find in the Old Testament.

THE FALL OF THE FIRST BEAST

When it came to kings, normally speaking, the throne or the position of rule was passed on from one generation to the next unless the king was without descendants or there was an event or revolt that caused a change in power. Even though the age of the monarchs lasted multiple millennia, monarchy came to its fall between the seventeenth and nineteenth centuries after absolutism swept through Europe.

Absolutism is, as the word says, an absolute form of rule by one person. To be an absolute monarch meant to have absolute power in a country or kingdom. There was no accountability—meaning there were no other individuals or bodies of government that were involved in the decision making. Kings during this time claimed that their power was supposedly given to them directly from God. If anyone opposed their rule, it was as if the offender was opposing God Himself. These types of rulers had existed throughout the entire era of kings, but absolutism became a lot more popular, whilst controversial, in the seventeenth and eighteenth centuries.

Across Europe and other parts of the earth, the oppression of the monarchs brought societies to a boiling point. Change lingered on the horizon, and the desire for freedom from monarchical rule came to the surface in the hearts and minds of men. This ushered in the age of revolution. Suddenly, people revolted in many nations and stood up violently against the monarchs.

The American Revolution and the French Revolution are perhaps the most well-known revolutions, but there were many other revolts and rebellions around the world. Most revolutions were in Europe, as it was the heart of the world at that time, but there were also revolutions in Asia and the Americas. Europe (the heart) was changed through revolution, and the world (the rest of the body) followed Europe's pattern.

IT HAPPENED IN THE SPIRITUAL REALM

I want you, the reader, to understand that this extreme and sudden change in the form of worldly governments happened because the dominion of the first beast was coming to an end. The natural change that is recorded in our history books happened because a prophecy that was written down in the books of all books, the Bible, was being fulfilled. The beast's lion heart was taken, and the beast's feathers were plucked. Its dominion was winding down, and the era of the kings was coming to an end.

"The first was like a lion, and had eagle's wings. I watched till its wings were plucked off; and it was lifted up from the earth and made to stand on two feet like a man, and a man's heart was given to it" (Daniel 7:4, NKJV).

It is amazing to think that what is recorded in Daniel 7:4 is exactly what happened to the monarchs in history. Their dominion over the people was plucked away from them by the revolting crowd. In the age of revolution, the ruler's elevated position over their people was eliminated. The kings were no longer hovering above the reach of their subjects, but a man's heart was given to each king, meaning their "god-like" status was taken away, and they were seen as any other mortal man. They were pulled down from their elevated palaces and thrones and set on their two feet.

"Made to stand on two feet like a man, and a man's heart was given to it" (Daniel 7:4, NKJV).

By making kings and queens mere men and women, the global pursuit of democracy was initiated. All of this is packed into the description of the first beast of Daniel's vision. Suddenly, every man had a voice. The rulers who behaved like lions and eagles were demoted. The age of revolution pulled them down from their sovereign state, plucked their feathers, and made them equal to all men.

Daniel wrote, "I watched till its wings were plucked off" (Daniel 7:4, NKJV).

The plucking of the royal's feathers was not just the symbolism in Daniel's prophecy speaking of the kings losing their elevated positions; the plucking of the feathers actually happened physically in those days. There were actual sympathizers of the monarchical rule who were tarred and feathered. After being tarred and feathered, the feathers had to be plucked from the bodies of the royal supporters. This brutal custom was first documented during the American Revolution and was not common at all in Europe or England. To this day, historians are still baffled by why and how this practice began. The first known incident of tarring and feathering was in the spring of 1766 during the American Revolution. John Gilchrist had a suspicion that British Captain William Smith had notified British authorities about his smuggling activities. In return, John and a few men tarred and feathered Captain William Smith for his support of the royal British crown. Another man named John Malcolm, who was also a loyalist and staunch supporter of the royal British crown, was also tarred and feathered publicly twice, once in 1773 and again in 1774. Tarring and feathering became more and more of a trademark of American revolutionaries.

Interestingly, the English royals had used the lion as an official symbol of their strength and power since the twelfth century, and suddenly, their supporters were being tarred and feathered. The question is where did the idea to do such a thing come from? What was the reasoning behind it? Nobody really knows the answers to these questions, but we do know that, in the book of Daniel, it is written, "I watched till its wings were plucked off" (Daniel 7:4, NKJV).

The American and French revolutions were the most dramatic of all revolutions. Great Britain and France were two mighty and vast monarchical empires. The French Empire completely imploded while the British Empire lost America, its biggest colony during those times of revolution. Both nations were never the same afterward. The change that the fall of monarchy and imperial rule brought to the world we live in is hard to put into words. To describe it as a milestone in world history would be a grave understatement. It is only fitting that Daniel's vision speaks of this change by foretelling the end of the first beast.

SILENCE BEFORE THE STORM

Throughout the nineteenth century, there were more revolutions, civil conflicts, and minor wars on the European continent, but overall, it was a rather peaceful time in Europe. I would call this time the silence before a terrifying storm. Even though the world had witnessed the fall of imperial France and the failed attempt of the British Empire to stop America's independence, there were still powerful nations that were under the rule of kings. The first beast did not lose its dominion in a matter of years but rather over a matter of centuries.

Over time, more and more European countries began to form democratic governments. Europe did not only change politically but also became engulfed in the Industrial Revolution, bringing technological, economic, and cultural changes. The Industrial Revolution swept across the European continent from Britain eastward. The way of life was rapidly changed and the way people approached life would never be the same. These industrial changes transformed not only the basic economies but also the weapon industries of many nations. A deadly race began to advance into the uncharted territories of technological superiority between each nation. There was not a free international market at the time, and nations even enacted laws that prohibited their citizens from selling new technologies to other nations. The unstable political climate and the promise of great profit fueled the ingenuity of the weapons industry. Suddenly, there were fighter planes, tanks, submarines, machine guns, artillery, and different kinds of poisonous gasses.

At the beginning of the twentieth century, tensions were brewing all over Europe. After the Austrian Archduke Franz Ferdinand was shot in Sarajevo, World War I began. This war started in 1914 and lasted until 1918. The First World War is often described as a mass slaughter rather than a war. Many civilians perished in the course of this war, and brutal battles were fought in endless trenches. Often, armies would not progress nor retreat an inch, and yet thousands of men died every day. All of the new technologies, weapons, and inventions available because of the Industrial Revolution were used in the war, making warfare far more brutal than any war ever before. After four years of grueling fighting and twenty million deaths, Germany, Austria-Hungary, Ottoman Turkey, and Bulgaria lost the war.

THE RUSSIAN REVOLUTION

The First World War triggered yet more revolutions. More kingdoms fell, more monarchs were turned into mere men, and more lions with eagle feathers were removed by the people. As Germany and Hungary were fighting against Russia, things began to shake within the Russian Empire. The monarchy led by Czar Nicholas II began to crumble because of stark economic instability and many defeats on Russia's western front. The general Russian population was suffering in severe poverty. There was a constant food shortage, and many life essentials were nonexistent. This all boiled up into intense wrath against Czar Nicholas II, and his once powerful regime fell like a house of cards.

The first beast was losing its grip worldwide, one nation at a time. The Russian monarchy fell, and another significant shift occurred in one of the most powerful nations on earth. A Communist government was instituted in Russia under Bolshevik leader Vladimir Lenin. Under Lenin, Russia changed, and Communist ideals were instituted nationwide for the first time in the history of this world. Russia left the battlefields of World War I behind, only to return years later to an even greater war.

Just as Russia's Czar Nicholas II faced a revolution after World War I, so did the German Kaiser Wilhelm II. After a rather short revolution, the German Empire became the German parliamentary republic, later known as the Weimar Republic. China, a nation that had been under monarchical rule for almost four thousand years, also turned into a republic in 1912.

Why all these historical facts? It is important to see the gravity of the change that the world went through and what was truly behind the change. For thousands of years, throughout every culture, the earth was ruled by long lineages of monarchs and rulers. Yet, within a matter of one hundred and fifty years, the entire world went through unprecedented changes politically, culturally, and technologically. It was as if a spiritual, unstoppable tsunami had swept across the globe. Think about it; with natural eyes, it is hard to fathom how all this happened. Logically speaking, it is easy to explain the revolution of one or two nations, but in order to explain all these revolutions and changes, some taking place in the most established nations on earth, a person needs to look at the spiritual realm. This shift manifested in the natural realm after it took place in the spiritual realm. The age of revolution and the fall of the monarchies happened because the dominion of the lion with eagle's wings was fading away, and a second beast was coming that would grab ahold of the world. Once again, Europe would take center stage, and once again, a major shift in the world would occur. This coming beast was the bear.

— CHAPTER 3: —
WE NEED SPIRITUAL EYES

WHEN THE NATURAL AND SPIRITUAL COLLIDE

We as Christians must always remember that behind any change in the natural realm, there must first be a change in the spiritual realm. Let me clarify. I am not saying that every little thing that happens in our natural lives has a spiritual root. For example, a tree might fall over in your garden today simply because the wind blew too hard and not because of some in-depth spiritual reason. What I would like to highlight, though, is that some of these big changes in world history or big changes in our personal lives happened because something shifted in the spiritual realm first. We as people are often so focused on the natural realm that we forget that life goes a lot deeper than what we can see with our natural eyes.

That is why Daniel's vision is so important. While biblical prophecy is not the only way that God uses to speak to us, it is definitely an important one. God gave us biblical prophecy so that we can understand the things that are happening around us. Daniel's vision shows us the spiritual realm, and the Holy Spirit connects the dots. He gives us revelation so that we can understand spiritually what is happening right before our eyes. Having a spiritual understanding is extremely vital. It shows us that God is in control, and it gives us discernment and wisdom on how to react.

As a pastor, I often sense things in the spirit in regard to the people that God has called me to take care of. When I say "I sense in my spirit," I mean that the Holy Spirit is communicating with my spirit. I might sense that there are problems that will arise over certain things or changes. I might sense a hard or a soft heart. I might sense a humble or prideful attitude, or I might sense a fiery or lukewarm attitude.

The moment I sense something in my spirit, I will start to react to what I am sensing. The things we sense in our spirit are a lot deeper than what we can sense in our soul or flesh, and God wants us to pay attention. Often, we must act on that sensing, with or without having natural evidence. That is where faith and sensitivity are required. If we are willing to be sensitive to the Holy Spirit and if we are willing to step out in faith, we will see a lot of spiritual fruit in our lives and in the lives of others. To see fruit is what the Christian life is all about.

As a pastor, God has called the elders of my church and me to be overseers of the flock. The word "overseer" does not mean "to lord over the flock" but "to watch over the members of the flock." The act of overseeing is a spiritual connection between the overseer and the member of the flock. Not too long ago, the Lord gave me a dramatic reminder of how serious the position as an overseer is and how important it is to react to what I sense spiritually.

There were two men who came to our church, and God was changing their lives. Both were growing in the Lord, and both had individual testimonies of God's saving grace and faithfulness. They were both committed to our church, and both were following God's will for their lives. One day, however, I sensed spiritually that both men were going to leave the church and that both men would stop following God's will for their lives. To my surprise, two weeks from then, my friends confirmed exactly that. I did not know this, but both men had, separately from each other, returned to their old sinful lifestyles. Both of them ended up in sinful things, and their actions damaged their relationships with many people in the community. In my spirit, I sensed that all this was happening without natural evidence. It was a dramatic reminder to me how important it is to be sensitive to the speaking of the Holy Spirit. Based on what I had sensed, I warned both individuals before they made these steps away from the Lord, but unfortunately, neither heeded my words.

Jesus gave us countless examples of how to follow the Spirit and why it is crucial to have spiritual eyes. In Mark chapter five, Jesus saw with His spiritual eyes that Jairus' daughter would be raised from the dead before it happened in the natural realm. He saw something that would begin in the spiritual and would manifest in the natural. In this portion of scripture, we can clearly see the difference between a carnal man's approach and Jesus' approach to the natural. The people saw the evidence in the natural world as final, but Jesus saw something else in the spiritual realm. He saw that girl being raised from the dead before it manifested in the natural. By the Spirit and by faith, which are both spiritual attributes, Jesus changed this girl's natural fate.

> While He was still speaking, some came from the ruler of the synagogue's house who said, "Your daughter is dead. Why trouble the Teacher any further?"
>
> As soon as Jesus heard the word that was spoken, He said to the ruler of the synagogue, "Do not be afraid; only believe." And He permitted no one to follow Him except Peter, James, and John the brother of James. Then He came to the house of the ruler of the synagogue, and saw a tumult and those who wept and wailed loudly. When He came in, He said to them, "Why make this commotion and weep? The child is not dead, but sleeping."
>
> And they ridiculed Him. But when He had put

them all outside, He took the father and the mother of the child, and those who were with Him, and entered where the child was lying. Then He took the child by the hand, and said to her, "Talitha, cumi," which is translated, "Little girl, I say to you, arise." Immediately the girl arose and walked, for she was twelve years of age. And they were overcome with great amazement.

Mark 5:35–42 (NKJV)

A few more things stand out to me about this passage. It is interesting that Jesus did not allow all of the twelve disciples to come with Him but only Peter, James, and John. Those three must have had greater sensitivity for the spiritual realm and more faith to see the girl rise from the dead. Jesus also removed all the doubters in the girl's house before raising her from the dead. He removed the people who were clinging to the evidence in the natural realm. People who allow unbelief are simply people who do not have spiritual eyes and ears. They are stuck in the natural realm and cannot understand the spiritual realm.

We also learn by reading this passage that if we choose to follow the Spirit rather than our natural eyes and understanding, we will also face ridicule and opposition as the people ridiculed Jesus. Always heed the Spirits' voice over the ridicule of the people. Always listen to what your spiritual eyes and ears are telling you. Do not let people pull you away from pursuing the spiritual kingdom. Remain persistent in regard to what you have sensed in the spirit. Trust His voice and, most importantly, act upon it.

Now we, brethren, as Isaac was, are children of promise. But, as he who was born according to the flesh then persecuted him who was born according to the Spirit, even so it is now. Nevertheless what does the Scripture say? "Cast out the bondwoman and her son, for the son of the bondwoman shall not be heir with the son of the freewoman." So then, brethren, we are not children of the bondwoman but of the free.

Galatians 4:28–31 (NKJV)

HEALTHY BALANCE

Not everything that happens around us will always be spiritual. There is a healthy balance. We live in a natural world, and in the natural world, natural things happen. If you hit your toe on a chair while walking through the house, there is most likely no deep spiritual meaning behind it. You simply did not see the chair, or you simply did not pay enough attention. Cars will break down, droughts will come, and injuries will happen. While things can have a spiritual cause, not everything has a spiritual reason behind it. Not everything is a spirit, demon, or enemy attacking you. Sometimes, life in the natural world just happens.

We must always listen to the Holy Spirit and not get caught up in an unbalanced approach. A person might not be paying attention while driving a car, and that person has a car accident. We cannot go around afterward and make big spiritual statements about the cause of the accident. On the other hand, a car accident could definitely be a spiritual attack or even the Lord trying to get our attention. In those cases, we must allow the Holy Spirit to reveal to us if there is something deeper happening and not just jump to conclusions. The wonderful thing about the Holy Spirit is that He will give us a gentle nudge. As long as we are sensitive to Him, there is a knowing deep inside of us that something else is going on. We must trust His guidance in this.

All of us must practice being sensitive to the Holy Spirit and learn how to listen to Him. We must train our spiritual eyes and ears. Most of us start this journey as spiritual brutes, and over time, testimony after testimony, we become like gentle doves, sensitive to the speaking of the Holy Dove. Once we have heard Him speak, we must then step out and do before the natural evidence appears or despite what the natural evidence tells us. He always goes first. As we step out in this, we will get to know Him better and better, and we will grow as spiritual Christians.

Jesus operated in this way, and so did the apostles. They did not wait for evidence in the natural realm, but they solely relied on the guidance of the Holy Spirit. Jesus knew by the Spirit that Judas would betray Him. He knew by the Spirit that Peter would deny Him. He knew by the Spirit that Lazarus had died before He was informed. He acted upon what He sensed by the Spirit, and often, the natural evidence came later. To be led by the Spirit requires sensitivity and faith. It also requires constant boldness and trust because we act upon what is not seen or not yet seen. John 3:8 (NKJV) describes walking in the Spirit perfectly: "The wind blows where it wishes, and you hear the sound of it, but cannot tell where it comes from and where it goes. So is everyone who is born of the Spirit."

Too many believers are living carnal lives with their focus only on natural things. Pardon my bluntness, but believers who are only focused on natural things are spiritually blind. They are blind, and so are their leaders who keep them in that state. True spiritual leaders will take a person who only lives in the natural realm and expand that person's horizons. True leaders make spiritual followers. We, as the body of Christ, cannot afford any more carnal churches. What we need is a spiritual awakening.

Whenever you meet a natural-minded believer, try to open their understanding with the help of the Holy Spirit and remind them that the Bible says to be spiritually minded. Some believers are open, and some are closed. Some will question you in order to understand, and others will question you to seed doubt. Once again, be sensitive to the guidance of the Holy Spirit. He might ask you to walk with a closed-off person for many years, or He may warn you to stay away from a person who simply wants to argue and cause unbelief.

"Leave them; they are blind guides. If the blind lead the blind, both will fall into a pit" (Matthew 15:14, NIV).

God wants us to have our eyes and ears open to spiritual things. This does not mean to be "so spiritual" that we are of no use in the natural world. It is actually quite the opposite. Even though God wants us to live by the Spirit, He does not mean for us to be useless in the natural realm. To live by the Spirit is practical and simple. Do not let anyone tell you that being spiritual means you can no longer function in the practical. The fruits of a spiritual person are evident in the natural realm. A spiritual believer's fruits are seen in his family, his work or business, and even in his appearance. To understand spiritual things is not hard or complicated but very simple because it is the Spirit who teaches us. Man's thinking often makes things more complicated than they should be. God is not found in complicated or confusing theories and concepts but in life-changing revelations that pertain to any person. Intelligent or less intelligent, poor or rich, educated or uneducated, strong or weak—to be a Spirit-led Christian is for everyone. So, with this understanding, let us look at the appearance of the second beast and what I believe is the historical and physical evidence of what happened in the spiritual realm.

— CHAPTER 4: —
THE SECOND BEAST–THE BEAR

THE RELEASE OF A BEAR SPIRIT

"And suddenly another beast, a second, like a bear. It was raised up on one side, and had three ribs in its mouth between its teeth. And they said thus to it: 'Arise, devour much flesh!'" (Daniel 7:5, NKJV).

The appearance of this second beast was marked by sudden wars and more changes in governments. Even though monarchy had been taken over by democracy in many parts of the world, the longing for total power would be the trademark of this second beast. This beast would not be held back by democracy; this beast would not allow democracy to bridle its ruthless power.

Under the arrival of the second beast, nations like Italy, Russia, Germany, and Japan were suddenly led by men with a strong urge for total power. These men were not kings nor democratic leaders, but they were dictators. They were very different from the other national leaders at the time. These men began to rule in the newly established era of democracy, and they were born during and after the fall of the first beast. Unlike democratic leaders, these men were not satisfied with the fruits of the new democratic age. They were not satisfied with democracy because what they wanted was total power. These men's names are very well known and have echoed again and again throughout the last century: Benito Mussolini, Joseph Stalin, Emperor Hirohito, and Adolf Hitler.

It is not a coincidence to see strong similarities in the way they ruled, their ambitions, and their behaviors. As the second beast appeared, its spirit was released over the world, and these men and their nations became recipients of its nature and purpose. They were vessels of its dominion. These men harnessed its power for a season and led the world into its most deadly and darkest hour, still unmatched to this day. Spurred on by this bear spirit, these four dictators pulled the rest of the world into a bloodbath. Millions of people died, and many experienced the dreadful power of the terrifying second beast.

RUTHLESS POWER

All the rulers under the first beast, the lion with eagle's wings, certainly had power and strong authority. There were certainly many gruesome kings, rulers, and leaders throughout all of history before the arrival of the second beast. However, there was something different about the four men who were under the spirit of the bear beast. These dictators were all known for their ruthless and merciless rule. Their ruthlessness was so extreme that even some of the most unbelieving and spiritually blind historians could only describe their behavior as demonic.

When we look at the animal, the bear, we see those same ruthless characteristics. A bear uses ruthless power and brutal force to kill another animal. Its claws and teeth are not sharp, so the bear is forced to kill by brute force, crushing, ripping, and tearing, exactly like those four dictators behaved throughout their years of power. There is also nothing sacred to the bear. Not even his own cubs or his own kind. The male bear, which is called a boar, is the number one killer of his own kind. No other animal kills more bear cubs than the bear itself. So it was with these dictators, as they killed many of their own people.

"And suddenly another beast, a second, like a bear. It was raised up on one side, and had three ribs in its mouth between its teeth. And they said thus to it: 'Arise, devour much flesh!'" (Daniel 7:5, NKJV).

The four dictators and their four nations devoured much flesh all over the world, killing more than sixty million people. They killed, imprisoned, tortured, and punished millions of their own countrymen. Even though nobody will ever know the exact numbers, many historians believe that Stalin himself killed approximately twenty million of his own kind. The Russian people suffered terribly under his regime. Executions, famines, and work camps were the norm for the thirty-three years of his rule.

Besides brutally murdering and slaughtering six million Jews, many of which were German nationals, Hitler also killed countless non-Jewish countrymen. He spread terror across the lands, and great darkness settled all over Europe and beyond. Also, Emperor Hirohito and Mussolini ruled in ruthless ways, and the blood of many innocent people was on their hands. Mussolini did not even show restraint within his own family, as he killed his own son-in-law.

DICTATORSHIP

Another characteristic of the bear is that it lives a solitary life. The bear does not hunt in packs but solely alone. After mating season, even the bears' mating partner becomes an enemy. The sow bear with its cubs is on constant alert since the boar will not only kill the cubs but, at times, also attempt to kill and eat the sow.

Stalin, Hitler, Mussolini, and Emperor Hirohito at first worked together. Germany, Japan, and Italy were allies and formed the Axis alliance. Germany had a nonaggression pact with Russia. Japan and Russia also signed a nonaggression pact. But despite all their pacts and alliances, all four leaders were ruled by the nature of the bear beast. They all ended up in war with each other.

Their drive for absolute power and rule was stronger than any pact or alliance. Hitler broke the pact with Russia and attacked Stalin's territory in 1941. Stalin broke the nonaggression pact with Japan in 1943 and attacked Japan in the Manchukuo State in 1945. Also, Germany and Italy's alliance did not stand. In 1943, Italy declared war on Germany. The only alliance that remained was between Germany and Japan. But this would have been just a matter of time. There was a great distance between the two nations, and they essentially fought two separate wars. Both nations surrendered before they interfered with each other's ambitions to rule the world.

We can clearly see the characteristics of the bear in all these four men. Their main pursuit was to achieve absolute control and power at any cost. Nothing was sacred, no partnership lasted, and their own people suffered the worst.

GERMANY—KILLING WHAT IS SACRED

While all four dictators committed horrible atrocities and together murdered millions of innocent men, women, and children, Hitler took on the characteristics of killing what is sacred to a heartbreaking extent. It is hard to even think about some of the crimes that were committed by Hitler and his Nazi party. I grew up in Germany, and to this day, when I enter Germany, I can still feel a heaviness over the nation. You can still see the guilt and the shame from Germany's past. The second beast led the entire nation of Germany into unfathomable hate and destruction. One of this beast's missions was to go after what was sacred, to go after what was holy, to go after God's people: the Jews.

IT WAS RAISED UP ON ONE SIDE

The second beast had dominion and purpose. Four nations and four dictators were overcome by this spirit, but it is important to state that its power and dominion were not distributed equally.

"And suddenly another beast, a second, like a bear. It was raised up on one side" (Daniel 7:5, NKJV).

Italy, Japan, and Germany could not prevail against Russia, which I call the true bear. In Daniel's vision, it says that this bear beast was raised up one side, meaning it was stronger on one side. I believe this raised-up side, this stronger side, speaks of Russia. History shows that Russia was more powerful than all three other nations, and Stalin triumphed over his three rivals. The three nations all had their clashes with Russia, but none of them could prevail.

Hitler's obsession to have power to dominate the world led him to a full-on attack on Russia, expecting a rapid victory. Russia was Hitler's natural enemy, and he wanted to use the Russian territory as a space to live for his Aryan race. Hitler expected to conquer the vast Russian nation as fast as other countries that he had invaded before. Italy, who was, at the time, still an ally of Germany, helped in the fight against Russia. Both nations worked together to come up with a plan on how to conquer Russia. They called it "Operation Barbarossa," and even though Germany and Italy succeeded at first, in a matter of twenty months, they had lost 60 percent of their soldiers. In April 1943, the Italian army had been decimated by the Russians and retreated back to Italy. The defeat in Russia was the beginning of Italy's road to surrender, which came to pass in September 1943.

The same was true for Hitler and Germany. His three-million-man army came to a screeching halt within twelve miles of Moscow in the deadly winter of 1942. After months of fighting, the German army retreated and lost the fight with the Russian bear. Russia invaded Japan's puppet state, Manchukuo, in 1945. The Red Army defeated the Kwantung Army of Japan, and historians agree to this day that this Russian victory aided in the surrender of Japan and, ultimately, the end of World War II.

Germany, Japan, and Italy all lost their fights against Russia.

Russia was vast, had a larger population, and was stronger. Daniel foresaw all of this in a vision when he saw that the bear was stronger on one side. It is incredible how accurate Bible prophecy is. These are not the only details in Daniel's vision that point toward Russia being the bear that was raised up. There are more details in his vision that describe Germany's defeat.

THREE RIBS BETWEEN ITS TEETH

"And had three ribs in its mouth between its teeth" (Daniel 7:5, NKJV).

Let us go back a few years. In the aftermath of World War I and the German Revolution, Germany became the Weimar Republic. In the Weimar Republic lived an author named Arthur Moeller. He wrote a book that was called *Das Dritte Reich*, which means "The Third Empire."

In his book, he advocates for a strong Germany that must not yield to the, at the time, prevalent Marxism nor to the new era of democracy. He claimed that both Marxism and democracy would hinder Germany from stepping up to a place of supremacy in Europe. His term "the Third Reich" refers to the two empires that had come before. The first "Holy Roman Empire" and the second "German Empire." His desire and appeal to the German people was to build a Third Reich, a third German Empire that would dominate Europe. Hitler took hold of Moeller's book and started to pursue and live out Moeller's vision about the Third Reich. Moeller himself would never see the Third Reich come to fruition as he committed suicide in 1925, an indication of the spiritual forces that were at work in Moeller's life, which I believe gave him the vision of a Third Reich.

After Hitler became chancellor in 1933, the term "Third Reich" was introduced, and more and more Germans accepted and celebrated it. It became the mission statement for Hitler and for Germany. The mission was to build the Third Reich and to achieve supremacy worldwide. While the German Third Reich certainly had power and dominion, there was one thing in its way: the Russian bear. I believe that the three ribs in Daniel's vision stand for the German Third Reich. Around ten years after Hitler's Germany became the Third Reich, he and Germany would find themselves between the teeth of the Russian bear, just like Daniel's vision tells us.

"And suddenly another beast, a second, like a bear. It was raised up on one side, and had three ribs in its mouth" (Daniel 7:5, NKJV).

Why does Daniel's vision specifically say rib bones? Rib bones are very different from any other bone in the human body. Ribs have the unusual ability to restore and regrow even when large portions are broken or damaged. To this day, researchers still have not fully figured out why rib bones have this unique ability. I believe it has something to do with how Eve was created. God chose to use a rib bone out of Adam's body to form Eve. Perhaps the rib bone has the special ability to regrow itself until today because God touched Adam's rib bone and formed Eve out of it. After all, we are all descendants of Adam and Eve.

What do the ribs stand for in Daniel's vision? Why would three ribs be a representation of the Third Reich? At the time of Germany's surrender in 1945, the country was in ruins. Important economic cities like the northern city of Hamburg, which had been home to the largest harbor in the world, were decimated to piles of rubble. During "Operation Gomorrah," the Allies had dropped nine thousand tons of bombs on Hamburg. The bombing was so intense that it created its own fiery tornado that swept through the city. The rest of Germany was in a similar shape. The infrastructure was nonexistent, the economy had collapsed, and the currency was worth nothing. The government was nowhere to be found, and the spirit of the Germans was in the gutters. Many of the young men who were needed to rebuild and repair the nation were either killed or crippled. Yet, Germany started instantly to rebuild and regrow with the help of America and its allies. Germany did not only regrow and rebuild itself to the point of simply functioning again, but it built itself back to a place that would exceed its former prosperity. By 1989, Germany had developed the third largest economy in the world and was called "Das Wirtschaftswunder" or, in English, "the German economic miracle."

This is not a coincidence; let us connect the dots. Just like the rib bone has the almost miraculous ability to regrow itself, Germany "regrew" itself from the fallen and destroyed Third Reich to the third most prosperous nation in the world. The year 1989, when Germany became the third largest economy, was the same year in which the Berlin Wall fell. The long and extensive Communist oppression in East Germany, which was instigated by Russia, finally ended. Think about that. The Third Reich's destruction began in World War II, with Germany finding itself between the teeth of the Russian bear. Then, in the same year in which Germany had fully "regrown," it left the mouth of the Bear. It could not be clearer that this is what Daniel's vision talks about. There is more in his vision that speaks of this.

THE BEAR'S TEETH

"And had three ribs in its mouth between its teeth" (Daniel 7:5, NKJV).

In Daniel chapter seven it does not say that the three ribs were in the bear's mouth, but the bear's teeth are specified. This is because the teeth are yet another confirmation of Germany being in Russia's mouth at the end of World War II.

There were two very significant, unusual, and mysterious weather situations that crippled the German army in their pursuit to conquer Russia. As the Germans were advancing on Moscow in October 1941, suddenly, the floodgates opened, and rain came down in sheets. Roads turned into deep mud. The precipitation became so severe that the Germans had to abandon motor vehicles, and even horses would get stuck in the mud up to their bellies. Foot soldiers had a hard time just walking. All this affected the forward progress of the German army in a drastic way. Germany had the upper hand at that moment, but because of the terrible road conditions, the German advance got stuck and ran out of ammunition, fuel, and other supplies. Their strategy was to overrun the Russians in a high-speed attack, but their advantage was taken from them by the weather.

It is common for it to rain in Russia at that time of the year, but the amount of rain in October 1941 was far more than was ever recorded before. This extreme shift in the weather could not have come at a worse time for the German army, and it brought their offensive to a screeching halt. This pause in their advance, however, could not have come at a better moment for the Russian army. The Russians used the time to send in new reinforcements and to fortify their positions in and around Moscow.

Next, the temperatures suddenly decreased. The mud began to freeze, and the rain turned into snow: a lot of snow. Despite the weather, the German army continued its offensive and headed for Moscow. Once again, another extreme weather condition stopped the German army at just the right moment. The temperatures continued to plummet and, just like the extremely wet fall, the winter of 1941–1942 became the coldest winter on record. The bitter cold paralyzed the German war machine yet again. Engines would not start, and rifles would not fire. The German soldiers were still dressed in their summer uniforms as temperatures hovered around minus forty degrees Celsius.

These two weather conditions are very significant. Many historians believe that if it had not been for this severe weather, Germany would have indeed conquered Moscow and most likely won its fight with Russia. The One who is in charge of the weather, however, made sure that Germany (the Third Reich) would end up between Russia's teeth, as recorded in Daniel's vision. You see, a brown bear typically has exactly forty-two teeth. It is not by chance that these two extreme weather events occurred and that in the year 1942, Germany lost the battle of Moscow and, with it, lost the momentum of Operation Barbarossa. This was the turning point in Germany's war with Russia.

— CHAPTER 5: —
THE BEAR AND THE CHURCH

THE EFFECT ON THE CHURCH

Before I get into the third beast, I think it is very important to highlight some of the spiritual changes that occurred during the dominion of the second beast. These are spiritual changes that are not recorded in our history books. Christian literature dramatically changed around the time of World War I and World War II. Three topics suddenly dropped out of Christian writings right around the time in which I believe the second beast rose to power. Coincidentally, these three subjects were the following:

1. Holiness
2. Sacrifice
3. Self-denial

Holiness, sacrifice, and self-denial are concepts that are not often preached about in today's church, but if we look in the scriptures, we find that all three are major pillars of the Gospel and the Christian life. They are major talking points of Jesus Himself. The very reason why these three topics dropped out of Christian literature during that time in history shows that the spirit of the bear did not just pull the nations into terrible dark days but sadly also affected the global church. Why would the spirit of the second beast go after these three topics? Because all three topics go exactly against the nature of the bear and ultimately against the nature of evil.

HOLINESS

To pursue holiness means to be on the road of sanctification. A person who pursues holiness does not look for the common or unclean things but the select treasures of a sanctified life. This person's journey is to be set apart from the world, refined and undefiled. It is really the journey that all of us, as Christians, are called to take. This journey begins the moment we are born again. From that moment forward, we are transformed from glory to glory if we allow God to work in our lives. Holiness is not something we can achieve in our own strength, but it is something that we can earnestly desire. A person who desires to grow closer to Jesus will automatically desire holiness because everything about Jesus is holy.

The bear represents the absolute opposite. The bear is an omnivore, just like the pig. It is an unclean animal, and there is nothing pure about the bear. If you look at the four dictators we discussed who were under the influence of the spirit of the bear beast, you can clearly see that there was nothing pure or sacred in their lives. All four dictators were against God and even into the occult and eastern religions. This spirit had a hold on these men and turned them all against the one holy God and His people.

To see such a stark shift in Christian literature away from holiness puts into perspective how powerful the second beast was. To this day, there are not many timely teachings about holiness in the church. I am sorry to say, but contemporary Christianity actually rejects the idea of holiness. People are encouraged to follow their own dreams and to live their best life now, while Jesus asked us to lay down our lives for Him.

"But just as he who called you is holy, so be holy in all you do; for it is written: 'Be holy, because I am holy'" (1 Peter 1:15–16, NIV).

"He has saved us and called us to a holy life—not because of anything we have done but because of his own purpose and grace. This grace was given us in Christ Jesus before the beginning of time" (2 Timothy 1:9, NIV).

Even though the spirit of the second beast has affected the church, it does not mean that it has authority over the church. It is up to the body of Christ, every local church, and every believer to understand our authority in Jesus and to walk in the authority that Jesus has given us. He has given us the power to overcome any spirit, and He has the keys to open any prison. This does not mean that we can change Daniel's vision about the beasts, but it means that we do not have to come under the beasts' rule. We can live lives under the rule of our rightful King Jesus.

SACRIFICE

Just like "holiness," the word "sacrifice" is a word that we do not hear often on Sunday mornings anymore. It is not a hot-selling topic in the Christian book industry either, but it sure is a very important topic in the only book that truly matters: the Bible.

The four dictators who were ruled by the bear spirit never sacrificed anything of themselves. They always took, but they never gave. What they took was never enough; they always wanted more until there was nothing more to give, and a whole continent was on the brink of absolute destruction. This ideology of taking and never giving goes exactly against the heart of the Gospel. To live the Christian life means to live a life of sacrifice. It means to love Jesus more than ourselves, to love our neighbors more than ourselves, and even to love our enemies.

"Greater love has no one than this, than to lay down one's life for his friends" (John 15:13, NKJV).

Jesus asks us to lay our lives down daily for the sake of the Gospel, for the benefit of our fellow Christians, for strangers, and, of course, for Himself. While we often hear to be kind and loving to our neighbors, how often do we hear in church to sacrifice something for someone else? How do we hear so little about sacrifice even though sacrifice is a foundational part of the Christian life and Christian love? To love someone often means to do something that will not benefit ourselves but rather the other person. To truly love means to sacrifice.

"And to love Him with all the heart, with all the understanding, with all the soul, and with all the strength, and to love one's neighbor as oneself, is more than all the whole burnt offerings and sacrifices" (Mark 12:33, NKJV).

God is not interested in external and materialistic sacrifices as much as He is interested in our internal sacrifices. At all times, He wants us to sacrifice our hearts' desires, our plans, and our dreams out of love for Him. To place our desires and our dreams on the altar of God can only come from a heart that truly loves Him. He wants us to give Him our whole hearts because half of a heart is not a sacrifice but a compromise. He wants to fill our whole being with His love and not just a portion of our being. If we do not sacrifice the things that are in the way, then it is impossible to love our neighbors as much as ourselves because a big part of our hearts is still beating for ourselves. We will always sacrifice something that is precious to us for what is more precious to us. Jesus must be, and become, the most precious treasure of our lives. If we do not give all of ourselves, the very part that we hold onto is the one thing that hinders us from loving like Jesus. He wants us to love just like He loves us, holding nothing back. This is impossible if a part of us is in self-preservation mode.

Jesus never lived in a self-preservation mode, but He laid down His life so that all people could find life. He desires for His followers to choose the same path that He did, as only such selfless love can conquer this dark world. The church must choose this path of sorrow again to make the impact that we are called to make. I encourage you, as the reader, to allow the Holy Spirit to help you to walk this selfless path, allow Him to comfort you, and guide you to live as Jesus did.

SELF-DENIAL

The character of the bear is to never deny itself but to go so far as to even kill its own offspring to preserve itself. Like I said before, the dictators who were under the second beast were just like bears. What began in the fleshly nature of those men moved quickly into the spiritual realm. They came under the bear spirit to such an extent that, at some point, that spirit had complete control. There was no more balance and no contentment. Their demonic selfishness was unbridled. The atrocities that they caused were beyond what a normal human being could commit and turned demonic. To this day, we still see the effects of the savage spirit that ruled over these men.

Unfortunately, the same lack of self-denial affected the church. "Self-denial" has become an almost exotic word and concept in the body of Christ. As I write this, I realize that in many churches I would be on very thin ice preaching this message, but I will continue to preach the message of self-denial as long as I live. I have learned that there is no blessing in being under the fear of men, but God's blessing comes only when we live under the fear of God.

It appears that this rejection of self-denial has really affected the church since the arrival of the second beast. Self-denial is a topic that has been subconsciously and unofficially banned in many churches all over the world. This is especially true of the Western church. We hear so much about how to follow our dreams, our desires, and our plans. We are told that Jesus wants to make us happy, and many of us treat Him like a vending machine. The Bible teaches that this earthly life is meant to be laid down for Jesus Christ so that He can build His kingdom here on earth through us. Nowhere does it say in the Bible that we will have an easy life, nor does it say anywhere that we are supposed to build ourselves a beautiful life on earth. The Bible teaches that our life here on earth should be focused on building God's kingdom and the reward that awaits us in eternity. Jesus said, "He who finds his life will lose it, and he who loses his life for My sake will find it" (Matthew 10:39, NKJV).

I myself had never heard about self-denial until I was almost twenty years old. Even though I went to church my whole life and attended churches all over Europe, North America, and even Africa, self-denial was a foreign concept for me as a young man. Today, I can tell you with certainty that there is absolute blessing and freedom in self-denial. I have discovered that only when I am in God's will am I truly free. There are many scriptures that talk about surrender and self-denial. The problem is that when a person is living a self-pleasing life, none of those scriptures are very appealing. What I like to tell people is that in order to understand surrender and to understand the blessedness of such a life, you first have to experience it. Surrender and self-denial lead to a beautiful life, but we will only understand and experience it on the other side of the eye of the needle.

All of us stand in front of the eye of the needle packed full of things that we want, things we think we need, and all the things that we have. In order to go through the eye of the needle, we need to give up all these things. Only then will we be able to pass through the eye of the needle and experience what a surrendered life is all about.

This type of life certainly does not sound fun, and the truth is that most Christians will run from this decision for most of their lives. But let me tell you, it is a glorious change when a person steps through the eye of the needle. On the other side awaits the fullness of God's love and countless blessings. God loves every person, but if our hearts are full of other things, then how can His love fully enter? Surrender is the door to a life full of love, rest, peace, and purpose. I pray more Christians will find the fullness of the Christian life and, by doing so, can leave fear, anxiety, and restlessness behind. It is the secret place of the Most High that the psalmist talks about that is found on the other side of the eye of the needle.

"He who dwells in the secret place of the Most High Shall abide under the shadow of the Almighty. I will say of the Lord, 'He is my refuge and my fortress; My God, in Him I will trust'" (Psalm 91:1–2, NKJV).

I myself am so thankful to the Lord that He has made me willing to let go of my will and my plans. Once I stepped through the eye of the needle, I never wanted to go back to the life I lived before. That being said, it is not a one-time decision but a daily decision, and I am learning to surrender more and more. The Bible says, in Matthew 6:33 (NKJV), "But seek first the kingdom of God and His righteousness, and all these things shall be added to you."

The truth is this: if you put Jesus first and surrender to Him, He will certainly bless you and, at times, even give you the desires of your heart. However, our motivation to surrender should never be to gain these things. No, we must surrender out of a heart devoted to Him. Our desire must be to simply please Him and follow Him first. If we only surrender in order to receive "all these other things that will be added to us," then our heart is in the wrong place. Jesus is first, and if He decides to bless us in return, it is up to Him.

Maybe you are reading this and are not willing to go through the eye of the needle. Maybe you are not willing to live a life of self-denial. Do not run from making this decision. If you are not willing, you can always ask the Lord to make you willing to live such a life. If you feel that you cannot pray to be willing, you can pray and ask the Lord to make you willing to be willing to live such a life. If you cannot even pray that, you can pray to the Lord to make you willing, to be willing, to be willing to live a life of surrender. He is faithful. The question is, are you willing to pray such a prayer?

Even as I am writing this, I am convicted and stirred inside to again and again lay my life down so that Jesus can live through me. "Lord make me willing in Jesus' name!"

— CHAPTER 6: —
THE LEOPARD WITH FOUR WINGS AND FOUR HEADS

THE THIRD REICH FALLS

Besides heavy losses for their army on the eastern front, Germany was also under heavy attack on the western front. The United States, who had entered the war in December 1941, had organized a full-scale military invasion. Together with British and Canadian forces, the United States attacked occupied France on June 6, 1944. Germany was now fighting a two-front war against the Americans, British, and Canadians on the western front and Russians on the eastern front. Month after month, the German armies were pushed further and further out of the territories that they had previously conquered. In the beginning of 1945, the invasion of the German homeland began. Not long after that, with his back against the wall, Hitler committed suicide. On May 7, 1945, Germany officially surrendered.

The Allied forces had prevailed, and Germany was defeated. The entire nation of Germany was lying in rubble. The political, economic, and cultural system of Germany was in ashes. Since Germany did not have a government or a leader, and because of the vast destruction, many thought that Germany had no more future.

Like many other European countries, Germany had been

through the rise and fall of the first beast: the lion with eagle's wings. Monarchy had gone from being dominant to obsolete. After the first beast, Germany was ruled by the second beast, the bear, only to be defeated by a stronger bear called Russia. The main purpose of this second beast had been fulfilled: much flesh had been consumed all over the world. Through fear, terror, and death, the bear had lived out the dominion that it had all over the world. Now, as the bear's era was coming to an end, another rule and yet another beast was on the horizon. And yet again, Germany would be strongly affected by this beast.

THE LEOPARD

"After this I looked, and there was another, like a leopard, which had on its back four wings of a bird. The beast also had four heads, and dominion was given to it" (Daniel 7:6, NKJV).

The beast that is described in Daniel's vision is a leopard with four wings of a bird and four heads. It is not clear if these heads are four leopard heads or four different animal heads. I believe that the leopard portion of this beast is a representation of the nation of Germany, while the four heads and four wings speak of four different nations. When I look at the leopard as an animal and identify this animal's characteristics, I believe it becomes very clear that the leopard in Daniel's vision is a representation of Germany.

1. Opportunistic: Leopards are naturally very opportunistic hunters. They exploit immediate circumstances. They wait for the right opportunity to benefit from a certain circumstance. In nature, that might mean a wounded animal, an older animal, or an animal that steps within reach. Leopards are constantly looking for the best odds to achieve a successful hunt.

2. Not Particular: Leopards are not particular about their prey, meaning they will hunt any animal, big, small, or even tiny. Their prey can be anything from a beetle to a large-bodied antelope. They will also hunt monkeys, fish, and even rats.

3. Ambush: Leopards stalk their prey and wait for just the right moment to attack. They like to hide in deep grass or on a tree and, from there, launch a surprise attack. This ambush approach makes the leopard's attack extremely quick and surprising for the prey. The prey has little to no time to react and save itself.

GERMANY'S OPPORTUNISTIC WARFARE

Germany fought Second World War just like a leopard would hunt its prey. The German Army Command was very opportunistic and strategic. Hitler and his generals correctly identified the weaknesses and strengths of surrounding nations and reacted accordingly. They picked the correct timing and approach to attack surrounding nations like France, Poland, and Russia. If it had not been for those two mysterious weather events, Germany would have won its war with Russia. The German plan to attack Russia speedily was, strategically speaking, a textbook approach to conquering such a vast and more populated nation. On the other hand, Hitler showed restraint in attacking nations like Switzerland, which had barricaded themselves deep into the Swiss Alps. Eventually, I believe Hitler would have also attacked Switzerland, but the small neutral nation was not of imminent interest to him. This highly opportunistic and strategic approach was completely different from the First World War, and a lot of nations became Germany's prey.

GERMANY'S ALL-CONSUMING WARFARE

Just like the leopard, Hitler was not particular about his prey. It is not a secret that he wanted to conquer the whole world, and he did not discard any nation in the process. Any nation that was conquerable and favorable to conquer, his German forces attacked to expand the Third Reich. Hitler was not picky; he conquered poor, wealthy, small, and large countries. Some countries possessed valuable resources and strategic locations, and other countries were a lot less valuable.

Germany's Ambush-Style Warfare

The reason why Germany was so successful in conquering such vast parts of Europe was because of its ambush-style approach. The German Army Command would stalk nations and then launch an extremely fast surprise attack. This form of warfare was brand new at the time and today is known as "Blitzkrieg" or "lightning war." The German army utilized tanks, airplanes, motorized infantry, and artillery to quickly push through enemy lines. Often, they succeeded in encircling whole armies, cutting them off from supply chains and reinforcements, which forced them to surrender.

THE FOUR HEADS AND THE FOUR WINGS

After Germany's defeat, the Allies knew that Germany would have to remain occupied. They did not want to see Germany react in the same way it had after World War I when it had become angered by the high reparations penalties and a crippled economy. Germany had become the perfect breeding ground for nationalism and the rise of the evil Nazi regime. The Allies feared that another war on the European continent could be instigated by Germany, so this time, they made sure that history would not repeat itself.

At the Yalta Conference in early February 1945, Great Britain's Prime Minister Winston Churchill, President Franklin D. Roosevelt, and Joseph Stalin decided to occupy Germany and divide it into four parts. After Germany's official defeat, it was split up into four parts. The Americans governed the southeast portion, the French the southwest, the British the northwest, and the Russians the northeast portion. Just as the nation was divided into four pieces, so was the northeastern capital, Berlin, sectioned out among the four nations. Let us look again at Daniel's vision and its description of the leopard.

> And suddenly another beast, a second, like a bear. It was raised up on one side, and had three ribs in its mouth between its teeth. And they said thus to it: "Arise, devour much flesh!"
> After this I looked, and there was another, like a leopard, which had on its back four wings of a bird. The beast also had four heads, and dominion was given to it.
>
> Daniel 7:5–6 (NKJV)

The leopard in Daniel's vision has four wings and four heads. Each wing on the Leopard's back symbolizes one of these four governing nations. A wing always gives direction, and it provides the thrust to follow a direction. That is exactly what the four nations provided for Germany. Each head in Daniel's vision speaks of each of these four governing countries that received a portion of Germany's capital, Berlin. A head speaks of decision-making, and the decision-making of a nation happens in its capital. These four nations occupied and governed the German capital, making decisions on behalf of Germany.

The division of Germany into four parts was the beginning of the rule of the third beast. It was also a signal to the nations of this world. A signal of dominion and power as the world watched how these four nations divided up their prey. They governed the head city of Germany, and the center of Europe. Yet, these four countries would display even greater dominion in the years to come.

DOMINION

"The beast also had four heads, and dominion was given to it" (Daniel 7:6, NKJV).

The first beast and the second beast certainly had dominion, but it was not explicitly mentioned in Daniel's vision like it was with the third beast. This is because the third beast was given greater dominion than the two beasts before it. The four nations of the third beast had more dominion than any kingdom of the first beast or any dictatorship of the second beast.

Consider this: the United States, Russia, the United Kingdom, and France were not just on the winning side of World War II, but they became the leaders of the world after World War II. If you look at these four nations' positions in the world since World War II, it is very evident that they stand out among the rest. This was yet another major spiritual shift that happened in the history of the world. It is truly amazing that all these dramatic spiritual changes were foretold in Daniel's vision.

International Dominion

"The beast also had four heads, and dominion was given to it" (Daniel 7:6, NKJV).

Throughout the last seventy-plus years, these four nations have been involved in every large-scale international decision. Their dominion is known all over the world. Despite being individual countries with individual interests, these four nations have governed this world. The United Nations (UN), perhaps the most powerful organization in the world, came into existence in 1945. The United States, Russia, the United Kingdom, and France were four out of the five founding nations, and today, their representatives hold four of the permanent Security Council seats.

Nuclear Dominion

Daniel's vision is incredibly accurate, considering what occurred at the end of World War II. These four nations' unchallenged dominion had much to do with the presence of a new weapon. A weapon that brought more dominion to its holder than any weapon in the history of the world before: the nuclear bomb. To this day, this weapon is still the most feared, the most destructive and deadly weapon on earth.

Imagine all the kings, rulers, and nations that had dominion throughout the history of the world: the Persian Empire, the Egyptian Empire, the Roman Empire, Alexander the Great, and Napoleon. Even though they had dominion over large parts of this world for extended periods of time, none of them ever possessed a weapon as powerful. The United States used this weapon when they dropped a nuclear bomb on Hiroshima to end World War II. The United States, Russia, the United Kingdom, and France were the first four nations to own nuclear weapons. That is why I believe it says in Daniel's vision that dominion was given to the Leopard. Currently, these four nations are among the top five countries that own nuclear weaponry.

Division Among the Four

At the beginning of their dominion during World War II, the four nations conquered aggressors Germany and Japan together. However, anything with more than one head is a monster. Things changed between the four nations in the aftermath of World War II. While all four nations received dominion, over time, they went in different directions and even began to oppose one another. Russia followed the Communist ideology, while the United States, Britain, and France remained capitalistic. This difference in ideology ushered in what is known as the Cold War.

The world held its breath while watching these superpowers flex their nuclear muscles. Surprisingly, throughout all the years of the Cold War, there was no active fighting between the four nations as they solely supported other nations to fight a proxy war. Is it not interesting that there never was any direct fighting between the four nations? Never before in the history of the world have there been opposing forces on such a scale that fought a proxy war for so many years. I believe it all goes back to Daniel's vision. These four nations were the heads and the wings of the third beast, and therefore, it was impossible to fight each other. They opposed each other, but they never eliminated each other. Otherwise, Daniel's vision would have said that the number of heads would have decreased.

Is the Dominion Coming to an End?

Over the last few decades, we have seen a decline in the dominion of these four nations. The international image of these four nations is not what it used to be. The economies of these four nations are not what they used to be. Russia stumbled first with the fall of Communism. The United States, France, and the United Kingdom have stumbled more and more in recent years. Foolish and unwise economic decisions have greatly weakened the once economic powerhouses. Political instabilities in all four nations have weakened their global dominion. The strong individual values of the three Western nations are not what they used to be, and America's outward image specifically has been crumbling for many years. The inward strength of these nations is dwindling, and it appears that their dominion is coming to an end. Other nations like China and the Arab league are on the rise. Could this mean that we are witnessing the end of the leopard? Could it be that we have already witnessed the end of the leopard? Could this mean that the fourth beast is coming? Or could it even be that the fourth beast has already arrived?

PART II: THE SPIRIT OF ANTICHRIST AND THE BEASTS

— CHAPTER 7: —
THE SPIRIT OF ANTICHRIST AMONG THE FIRST BEAST

MANY ANTICHRISTS HAVE COME

Before we can proceed with the interpretation of the fourth beast, we must understand that there is a difference between the spirit of Antichrist, antichrists, and the final Antichrist. The spirit of Antichrist has raised up many antichrists throughout the history of this world. He has done so by entering willing human vessels like Adolf Hitler. These men, however, were just antichrists. Their lives, their legacy, and their actions show an absolute hatred for God and anything godly, but their rule and power were limited. At the end of the age, however, the spirit of Antichrist will raise up the final Antichrist, who, for a season, will rule without limitation. He will be more powerful, fully unbridled, and will rule over the entire earth instead of only certain territories like the antichrists that came before him.

"And every spirit that does not confess that Jesus Christ has come in the flesh is not of God. And this is the spirit of the Antichrist, which you have heard was coming, and is now already in the world" (1 John 4:3, NKJV).

"Little children, it is the last hour; and as you have heard that the Antichrist is coming, even now many antichrists have come, by which we know that it is the last hour" (1 John 2:18, NKJV).

Under no circumstances do we, as believers, want to be tricked by this spirit, nor do we want to give it any room in our lives. This spirit is very sneaky and is absolutely deadly, leaving a trail of destruction throughout history. To gain some understanding of the final Antichrist let us look at the work of this Antichrist spirit throughout history.

A TRAIL OF DESTRUCTION

The spirit of Antichrist has been around for a long time and has left a trail of destruction throughout the ages. During the life of Jesus, this spirit's purpose was to go against Jesus and kill Him, starting at the time of His birth. We know that when Jesus was yet a little baby, King Herod attempted to kill Him. This was that very spirit of Antichrist manifesting itself through King Herod. This spirit drove King Herod to such hate that he ordered soldiers to kill every boy under the age of two. Imagine the terror and suffering the people must have gone through. Mothers were wailing and weeping everywhere because this spirit caused Herod to murder innocent babies to stop Jesus. Even the prophet Jeremiah prophesied of this terrible event.

"Then was fulfilled what was spoken by Jeremiah the prophet, saying: 'A voice was heard in Ramah, lamentation, weeping, and great mourning, Rachel weeping for her children, refusing to be comforted, because they are no more'" (Matthew 2:17–18, NKJV).

This was the first time that this spirit manifested itself by using a member of the Herod family, but it was certainly not the last time. After King Herod, known as "Herod the Great," died, his son Herod Antipas took over and was used by the very same spirit. He was the man who killed John the Baptist, the very man who spoke of the coming of the Messiah and who prepared the way for Jesus.

Then later, Herod Antipas mocked Jesus during His deadly trial. The Bible says that Herod Antipas and his men of war mistreated Jesus and dressed Him in a purple robe to cause Him shame.

This spirit succeeded when Jesus went to the cross, but it is important to state that this spirit only succeeded in killing the body of Jesus because Jesus and the Father allowed it for a far greater cause: the salvation of mankind. The spirit of Antichrist was working among the very crowd that assembled in front of Pilate when he asked them if they wanted Barabbas or Jesus to get crucified. It persuaded the multitudes to call out for the crucifixion of an innocent man over the crucifixion of a convicted criminal.

After Jesus' resurrection and ascension, its focus shifted from stopping Jesus to coming against anyone who follows and glorifies the Son of the living God. This spirit goes after Christians, Christian values, and the Christian church worldwide. One of its tactics is to build an opposing kingdom of darkness to combat God's kingdom here on earth. This spirit spreads filth in order to combat holiness, and it seeds corruption in order to stall sanctification.

After Herod Antipas came "Herod Agrippa the First," who imprisoned Peter in order to stop the spreading of the Gospel. The Bible tells us that Herod Agrippa would not give glory to God when men called him a god, so an angel of the Lord struck him immediately, and he died. It is interesting that God did not allow "Agrippa the First," who was influenced by the spirit of Antichrist, to blaspheme God, but that He will allow the final Antichrist to do so for a season. I believe that the full wrath of God went after Herod Agrippa because that spirit blasphemed God before its permitted time. When the final Antichrist will rule and speak pompous words against God, he will only be able to do so because God will allow him to do so for a season, but more on this later. Looking at Agrippa's end, we are getting a taste of how God will deal with the final Antichrist at the end of time. God will destroy him and take away his dominion forever.

This Antichrist spirit was active in the era of each beast, and its power has intensified with every beast. During the dominion of the first beast, there were many wicked kings and rulers like the Herod line. No one, however, came even close to the evil emperor Nero. The spirit of Antichrist infiltrated that man's heart and mind and used him to persecute many Christians. The timing of Emperor Nero's rule was no coincidence but was Satan's strategic response to the birth of the church. After the day of Pentecost, the Gospel was spreading like a glorious wildfire from north to south and east to west. In an attempt to stop the global church from growing and making Jesus famous, the devil released the spirit of Antichrist upon the most powerful kingdom on earth at the time: the Roman Empire. Emperor Nero, at the empire's helm, turned into the cruelest and most evil ruler under the first beast. To this day, historians are baffled about the wickedness that came out of this man. He murdered his own mother and siblings so that he would inherit the throne.

Once fully in power, emperor Nero turned against the Christians with unprecedented hate and vigor. Any Christian who would not renounce their faith in Christ was publicly executed. At times, this meant that these saints would face dogs, lions, and other wild animals in the coliseum, being eaten alive in front of spectators. At other times, he would brutally crucify Christians. Nero would also use Christians as human torches, covering them in tar to be burned alive in the streets of Rome, lighting up the city at night. It is no coincidence that both Paul and Peter were killed by Emperor Nero. These two men were foundational pillars of the early church, and the spirit of Antichrist, through Nero, succeeded in killing them. Its focus was to stop the church's growth in order to tame the fame of Jesus Christ.

None of this, however, stopped the church from growing. No matter how cruel and gruesome the persecution of those early believers became, they did not stop preaching the Gospel. Instead of diminishing, Christianity actually spread fervently across the entire Roman Empire, converting it one soul at a time. At age thirty, Nero committed suicide after Rome turned against him in response to his terrible rule. Even after Nero's rule, there were many emperors who persecuted Christians, but in AD 313, all of this changed. Christianity became legal under Emperor Constantine I. After this, the Roman Empire became a Christian empire, and Constantine himself converted to Christianity at the age of forty.

With the powerful Roman Empire turning to Christianity, the Gospel now spread faster and further than ever before. By the end of the dominion of the first beast, Christianity was the prominent religion in the Western world and was spreading to other parts of the world.

THE SPIRIT OF ANTICHRIST AND ISLAM

When the devil realized that he could not stop the spread of Christianity by persecuting and murdering Christians, he added a different approach to his repertoire. He released the spirit of Antichrist to fabricate new religions. These religions would preoccupy the hearts and minds of millions of people. Through this, Islam was born.

My intention is not to insult any person from another religion, but it must be said that the very foundation of Islam is primarily against Christianity. Without going into too much depth on this subject, it is important to point out the truth about the origin of Islam. Their prophet Muhammad claimed that he had received a divine revelation about the "true god" in the seventh century, over six hundred years after the death and resurrection of Jesus.

After receiving his vision, Muhammad proceeded to share his teachings with Christians, but they rejected them. He then turned to the Jews, thinking that they would certainly come and join him since the Jews did not agree with the Christians about Jesus being the Messiah, but the Jews also rejected his false teachings. Muhammad was writing the Quran from AD 610 until his death in AD 632. Note that the Bible was written by many godly men; the Quran, however, was written by only one man and is based on one man's vision.

Islam, however, is not just a counterfeit religion; it also has become the one religion that stands strongly against Christianity. Today, Islam is the second most practiced religion in the world, and the countries under its full grip are completely closed to Christianity. Any Muslim who converts to Christianity in those nations is executed. The persecution of Christians in those countries is the most vicious of all the countries of the world. This is not a coincidence but is the very handwriting of the spirit of Antichrist.

A few years ago, I was invited to go to a certain Muslim nation in Asia to preach the Gospel. As I got to know the pastor, I realized how much hate the Muslims there have toward Christians. I saw a video in which men from his church pulled the body of a five-year-old girl out of a dirty sewer. Days before, the girl had been abducted from her home by several Muslims. Before they drowned the girl, the adult men raped her. This they did to openly demonstrate their power over Christians and to cause Christian families open shame. This is not a singular event, but these forms of persecution happen all over the Muslim world. Sadly, we have become somewhat accustomed to the reports of the killing of Christians all over the world.

This can only be the spirit of Antichrist in action. It is ruling an entire religion, an entire part of the Eastern world. Only a spirit could make people commit such evil deeds. Only a spirit could cause people to commit suicide in order to kill other innocent civilians and, in the same breath, convince them that they will receive a reward for such a deed.

Did you know that Muslims believe that Jesus walked on this earth, that He was born to a virgin, and that He performed many miracles here on earth? Here is where Muslims believe differently than Christians. According to the Quran, Jesus was just a prophet. Muslims believe that Jesus was not crucified but simply ascended to heaven as a prophet. Why does the spirit of Antichrist permit Muslims to believe that Jesus was a prophet and that Jesus walked this earth? Because there is no power in those two beliefs. There are many godly prophets in the Old Testament who do not affect our lives today. Jesus, however, was not just a prophet. The power of His life is based on the undeniable fact that He is the only begotten Son of God, that He was sinless and perfect, that He died for us on the cross, and that He rose from the grave. To deny these truths about Jesus Christ is the working of the spirit of Antichrist. This Spirit knows that the moment a person realizes that Jesus is not just a prophet but the Son of God who died for us is the very moment that salvation begins.

Today, Islam is one of the most powerful manifestations of the spirit of Antichrist and comes directly against Christianity and Judaism. On the famous Al-Aqsa Mosque, which is located in the temple area in Old Jerusalem, we find two descriptions that state, "God does not need a son." It is not called "the spirit of Antigod" but "the spirit of Antichrist" for a reason. This spirit goes against the Christ, the Messiah, the Lamb of God, the only hope for sinners like you and me to find salvation.

CHAPTER 8:
THE BEAR AND THE SPIRIT OF ANTICHRIST

A NATION OPENS ITS GATES TO HELL

The war between good and evil did not only continue after the era of the first beast, but it actually intensified. The spirit of Antichrist still had the same mission and was sent to bring more destruction and evil than ever before. With each beast, the spirit of Antichrist grew in strength. Even though this spirit operates worldwide, it appears to, at times, focus on one specific nation. This time, it was not the Roman Empire but the German Empire.

It is important to note that Germany only became a unified empire in 1871. Before the unification, there was the German Confederation, which consisted of many German-speaking kingdoms and sovereign states: the Kingdom of Prussia, the Kingdom of Bavaria, the Kingdom of Hannover, and so on. These German-speaking states, which later became the German Empire, were at the time culturally and economically very influential to the rest of Europe, similar to the Roman Empire at the height of its rule. The devil does not attack by chance, but he always attacks strategically. I believe that the devil sent his Antichrist spirit and purposefully infiltrated Germany in those years. This was a strategic move and was made possible because Germany had its guard down and its spiritual doors wide open. Let me explain:

When a person falls into sin, oftentimes, they are surprised. They say to themselves, "I didn't see that coming..." While that person perhaps did not see it coming, there is no doubt that the devil did not only see it coming but planned it that way. The Bible tells us that the devil always tries to ensnare us in sin. Just as a trapper knows the patterns of his targeted animal, so does the devil know our weaknesses and fleshly tendencies. A trapper will often set up an attractive bait that is made specifically for the animal that he is after. He will let the animal come in and feast on the bait. Time and time again, these animals come to the bait, and they become comfortable around it. Once they have made trails to the bait, the trapper will set up nearly invisible snares on each of the trails that the animal made. The next time the animal comes in to feed on the bait, it runs right into the loop of the snare and is caught. The same concept is true when it comes to our fleshly nature that leads to sin. The devil wants to ensnare us in sin. He wants us to get comfortable with our fleshly desires. He wants our conscience to become dull, just like the senses of an animal who comes into the same bait over and over again.

"Therefore we also, since we are surrounded by so great a cloud of witnesses, let us lay aside every weight, and the sin which so easily ensnares us, and let us run with endurance the race that is set before us" (Hebrews 12:1, NKJV).

Gideon was a prime example of this. He was so hesitant and unsure of following God. He had a great deal of insecurity in himself. He needed the visitation of an angel and two miraculous signs before he did what God told him to do. Later in life, just before he fell into massive sin, he did not inquire of God even one time, nor did he ask for a sign before committing that grave sin. He did not check if what he wanted to do would please God. He comfortably followed his fleshly desires and fell into idolatry.

"Then Gideon made it into an ephod and set it up in his city, Ophrah. And all Israel played the harlot with it there. It became a snare to Gideon and to his house" (Judges 8:27, NKJV).

Just like these trapped animals, our fleshly desires and the devil's temptations are often what lead us into deep sin. Once we are ensnared in sin, there is no guarantee that we can make it out. The Bible actually tells us that we must resist the devil to overcome temptation and sin. While God's grace today is still ever sufficient for us, we must never forget that our will to overcome sin is a vital part of being free of it.

"Therefore submit to God. Resist the devil and he will flee from you" (James 4:7, NKJV).

So remember, the enemy is always looking for open doors and empty spaces to occupy. That is exactly what happened with Germany. The nation's doors were wide open, and Germany was not occupied by God. Any person, any group of people, and any nation that does not belong to Jesus Christ is easy prey for the enemy. Once upon a time, this great nation of ours, the United States of America, confessed boldly and united to be "one nation under God." Protection and blessing were showered upon us because of this powerful confession and the belief in God that came along with it. Just like it is happening today in this great nation, the German-speaking nations back then turned further and further away from God.

The open embrace of Western philosophy, which is rooted in Greek mythology, was one of many open doors for Germany. This door was not just cracked open, but it was wide open. The country that called itself the nation of "poets and thinkers" fully embraced and sometimes even worshiped these poets and philosophers with atheist voices. Several of the most famous and most celebrated German writings come from the seventeenth, eighteenth, and early nineteenth centuries and are full of the occult, paganism, Greek mythology, and atheism. Let me give you an example. The most celebrated German writing is called *Faust*. Johann Wolfgang von Goethe wrote it in 1806 and 1808. This two-part drama is to this day considered Germany's "greatest contribution" to world literature. The story of *Faust* is about a man (Faust) who makes a pact with the devil in order to seduce a teenage girl. This teenage girl then kills her own mother to have more privacy for sexual relations with Faust. The girl becomes pregnant, and after giving birth, she then kills the baby.

Really? And this is, to this day, the most celebrated German writing? Can you see that something must be spiritually off for a nation to celebrate such filth? Even in today's crazy culture, I could not see any normal society praising such disgusting writings, but if you think about the fact that this was written over two hundred years ago in a far more God-fearing world, it makes it even harder to comprehend. How could a so-called "Christian" country align itself with such writings? The spirit of Antichrist.

It comes as no surprise that the writer Goethe himself was a Freemason and had a connection to the Illuminati. Writings like *Faust* were not rare but became very popular and frequent in German culture. For example, Friedrich Wilhelm Nietzsche also had a strong following and was celebrated in the German-speaking realm. This man was clearly demon-possessed as he challenged truth in itself and publicly expressed his hatred for God. The nature of people is shown by what they identify with and what they celebrate. For a nation to celebrate Nietzsche shows its colors and tells us that there was something deeper at work, something darker. There are many quotes of Nietzsche expressing his admiration for other religions and, in the same breath, his hatred for Christianity:

"For this remains as I have already pointed out the essential difference between the religions of decadence: Buddhism promises nothing, but actually fulfills, Christianity promises everything, but fulfills nothing."[1]

"If Islam despises Christianity, it has a thousandfold right to do so: Islam at least assumes it is dealing with men."[2]

"I call Christianity the one great curse, the great intrinsic depravity."[3]

There are many more evil quotes like this and many more German poets and thinkers who followed the same train of thought. The nation that had at one time birthed the reformation now celebrated men like Goethe and company. Nietzsche himself reaped the reward of his poisonous words and writings long before his death as he was plagued with many terrible diseases. He eventually turned insane, lost his mind, and died.

Why am I telling you about these men and their fame in Germany? Because I want you, the reader, to see the spiritual climate of the German-speaking nations. Goethe, Schiller, Nietzsche, and their colleagues were the flagships of a movement that was started by the spirit of Antichrist. This spirit used them and many other cultural changes to bring unbelief and atheism to the German-speaking nations. This was not just a trend of a fringe group, but it was an entire movement that went through the German-speaking nations and other parts of Europe. Officially, this movement is known as the Age of Enlightenment. The three main points of this movement were reason, skepticism, and individualism. At first glance, it is easy to see that the three pillars of that movement stand proudly against the almighty God.

1. Reason: "To reason" means "to use the natural mind," which the Bible says is in enmity with God. The act of rea-

---

[1] Friedrich Nietzsche, *The Antichrist* (1895).
[2] Friedrich Nietzsche, *The Antichrist* (1895).
[3] Friedrich Nietzsche, *The Antichrist* (1895).

soning leads a person to believe only what the natural eye can see and the carnal mind can grasp. Therefore, a reasoning person will not put their trust and faith in the living God who cannot be seen and who logically may not always make sense.

"Because the carnal mind is enmity against God; for it is not subject to the law of God, nor indeed can be" (Romans 8:7, NKJV).

2. Skepticism: Skepticism is nothing else but unbelief. It is one of the most powerful weapons of the devil. Unbelief is a deadly seed from the enemy. It is important to understand the danger of this seed. If any person embraces this seed and lets it grow, that same person will be spiritually robbed. The end result will always be spiritual death.

"Take heed, brethren, lest there be in any of you an evil heart of unbelief, in departing from the living God" (Hebrews 3:12, KJV).

3. Individualism: The desire for individualism is the desire to be independent. Independence from God was part of the first sin in the garden of Eden. It was there that the devil tempted Eve to become independent through knowledge. As a follower of Christ, we are called to be fully dependent on God in everything. We are fully reliant on His grace and His finished work on the cross. Individualism and independence are snares from the devil. He attempts to lure people in with a counterfeit idea of freedom.

My soul, wait silently for God alone, for my expectation is from Him. He only is my rock and my salvation; He is my defense; I shall not be moved. In God is my salvation and my glory; The rock of my strength, and my refuge, is in

God. Trust in Him at all times, you people; Pour out your heart before Him; God is a refuge for us. Selah. (Psalm 62:5–8 NKJV).

Can you see that the Age of Enlightenment was founded on the same pretense that Satan offered Eve? First, he brought skepticism by asking Eve, "Has God indeed said, 'You shall not eat of every tree of the garden'?" (Genesis 3:1, NKJV). He then sowed reason and individualism by saying, in Genesis 3:4–5 (NKJV), "You will not surely die. For God knows that in the day you eat of it your eyes will be opened, and you will be like God, knowing good and evil."

Eve opened the doors of her heart and mind and allowed the devil to steal her place of protection, belonging, blessing, and unity with God. Just like Adam and Eve, the German-speaking nations and other nations in Europe opened the door to the devil throughout the Age of Enlightenment.

The spirit of Antichrist used intellectual, unbelieving men to reason God away, and a nation that desired to be independent of God gave ears to their words. Instead of bringing actual light, the Enlightenment movement brought utter spiritual darkness to Europe. The Germans and the French, in particular, embraced this enlightenment ideology above other nations. What came was not just a gentle shift but a strong departure from God with dire consequences.

GERMANY, THE BIRTHPLACE OF COMMUNISM

Right after the Enlightenment period, Karl Marx, the founding father of Communism, was born in 1818 in Trier, a city in German-speaking Rhineland-Palatinate. The city of Trier is the oldest German city and dates all the way back to the Roman Empire. Marx's parents were of Jewish descent but dropped their religious beliefs because of the German society's views against the Jews.

Karl Marx was a heavy drinker from an early age. His drinking and smoking were so severe that he developed a weak chest, and the military rejected him for service when he was only eighteen years old. Throughout his life, he suffered from continuous eye inflammation, rheumatic pains, constant headaches, insomnia, nervous disorders, persistent boils, and recurring abscesses, which were so bad that he could not even sit down. He himself described all these illnesses as his "wretchedness of existence."

Marx became a strong atheist, and his comment, "Religion is the opium of the people," became known worldwide. Opium is a strong pain medication with highly addictive properties. In other words, he was saying, "Faith in God is not real but just something that distracts a person from the pains of life." The church, in Marx's opinion, was just a social institution to distract people from their suffering here on earth.

It is very important for us to understand the heart of Karl Marx and his colleague Friedrich Engels, who together wrote *The Communist Manifesto*. These two men were the founding fathers of a deadly ideology that killed and destroyed millions of lives. Both men were staunch atheists who hated God and anything holy. While it is indeed hard to put into words the utter destruction that Communism has brought upon this world, it is very easy to see the spirit of Antichrist in this ideology called Communism. Such death and such evil fruit can only come from a spirit from the kingdom of darkness.

It is hard to ignore the fact that both Marx and Engels died of illnesses in their throats. Marx died of bronchitis, and Engels died of throat cancer. Perhaps the cause of their deaths is a sign of the nature of all the evil words and deception that came out of them. When you look at the life that Karl Marx lived, it is clear to see that he reaped what he had sown. The devil will use people who open themselves up to him, but he will not spare them nor protect them.

He plays them like a fiddle, but he hates them as much as any other person created in the image of God.

Communism, to this day, is in its very nature against God. Aspects of it are packaged in an appealing way: a way that can even seem caring. However, Communism's expressed care for the lesser fortunate class is just a disguise. The spirit of Antichrist not only packaged atheism into Communism but also created, in some ways, a counterfeit of Christianity.

"Pure and undefiled religion before God and the Father is this: to visit orphans and widows in their trouble, and to keep oneself unspotted from the world" (James 1:27, NKJV).

Pure and undefiled religion is to take care of the weak and overburdened. God wants us as Christians to take care of widows, orphans, and the poor, as it is a powerful testimony of God's never-ending love. The devil knows this. He also knows that the unsaved world reacts with an open heart to these acts of love, so he used his main tactic and created a counterfeit for God's system. Martin Luther King said that in taking care of the weak and poor, Communism directly competes with Christianity. For this very reason, he called Communism "Christianity's only rival." Communism pretends to care about the poor and the weak. But history shows that the weak and poor have always suffered the most under any Communist regime. This is because Communism, in itself, goes against God's order. It is not inspired by God's love for the needy, but it exploits the weak and the needy.

Even though the spirit of Antichrist had worked in Germany through Marx and Engels by inspiring them to write *The Communist Manifesto*, this spirit was not yet satisfied. Communism was still in its birthing stage, and it would take several decades to gain traction. Germany, indeed, was the nation that birthed Communism, but it would not be the nation that would run with it. The spirit of Antichrist had different plans with Germany…

PERGAMON, THE ANCIENT PLACE OF THE THRONE OF SATAN

"I know your works, and where you dwell, where Satan's throne is. And you hold fast to My name, and did not deny My faith even in the days in which Antipas was My faithful martyr, who was killed among you, where Satan dwells" (Revelation 2:13, NKJV).

In the book of Revelation, we read about the seven letters to the churches. One of those letters is directed to the church in Pergamon. The ancient city of Pergamon was the center of pagan worship in Asia Minor. Located in this city was the altar of Zeus, which was also known as the throne of Satan. After many wars and natural disasters, the city was destroyed, and many artifacts were covered and forgotten. Before its destruction, the city of Pergamon was known for its literature, art, science, and technology, just like the German-speaking nations later on.

The man Antipas, who is mentioned in Revelation 2:13, was a bishop who was appointed by John the apostle in the city of Pergamon. During Emperor Nero's reign, Antipas was executed by the pagan priests of Pergamon. They offered him as a sacrifice on the altar of Satan by burning him alive.

THE THRONE OF SATAN COMES TO GERMANY

In 1871, the German Empire was founded, and all of the separate states and kingdoms came together under one name, one government, and one flag. After the German Empire was founded, the new leadership believed that the German Empire had to match the cultural advancements of the surrounding empires. Two men named Carl Humann and Alexander Conze were charged with the excavation of the Pergamon Altar, which was at the time located in the Ottoman Empire. In 1878, excavation began, and by 1879, the first pieces of the Pergamon Altar, the throne of Satan, arrived in Berlin, the German Empire's capital. A museum was built, and the Pergamon Altar was first publicly displayed in 1901. By 1930, a new museum was built for the sole purpose of displaying the Pergamon Altar in its entirety.

In its ancient place, the Altar of Pergamon was the altar of Zeus, and it was dedicated to the goddess Athena. A massive statue was built on the east side of the altar depicting the goddess Athena with a massive snake on one side. When Alexander Conze left the University of Vienna in 1877, he received a bronze medal for his work. This medal showed on one side a portrait of Alexander Conze, but on the other side, it depicted the goddess Athena from the Pergamon Altar. The strange thing is that Alexander Conze had not yet even started the excavation in Pergamon, nor would he have had any idea that this statue would be there when he received this medal. This statue of the goddess Athena was found at the end of 1880. Before this, only descriptions and small replicas were known to people. Conze's medal showed his future before it ever happened.

Allow me to recap here for a moment. The German states and kingdoms embraced the Age of Enlightenment and opened their doors to the occult, Greek mythology, paganism, and philosophy. After the period of enlightenment ended, *The Communist Manifesto* was written in Germany, and right after the founding of the German Empire, the Altar of Pergamon, which is described as the throne of Satan in the book of Revelation, gets excavated and brought to the German capital. You can see that all these things did not happen by coincidence, but something larger was at work, something darker. This dark force was using this nation to bring great darkness to the world. The spirit of Antichrist was operating in the German Empire in plain sight, and it had only just begun.

WE NEED THE HOLY SPIRIT

What always shocks me the most about this period in time is that right after the throne of Satan came to Berlin, it was the church of Germany that decided to open the gates of hell even further.

In the Bible, we read how Jesus promised us that the gates of hell would never prevail against His church. That is true for a passionate church that follows God's will, but is it true for a church that, in many ways, has departed from God and aligned itself with an unbelieving society?

For many decades up to this point, the German people, society, and even the German church had conformed themselves more and more with the world. The spirit of Antichrist had successfully shaken fundamental parts of the Christian society. The nation that once had fathered men like Martin Luther and Gutenberg became friends with this world, even though the Bible tells us to be separate from the world.

It says, in Romans 12:2 (NKJV), "And do not be conformed to this world, but be transformed by the renewing of your mind, that you may prove what is that good and acceptable and perfect will of God."

The German-speaking nations and states had been and still are famous for their great theologians. Theology simply means "God-thought," and in many ways, theologians are able to explain God and the essence of the Gospel in a logical way, which is good and very needed. But there is more to God and His ways than what we can muster up in our own thinking. A true theologian, a true teacher of the Word, is someone who does not teach merely information but who teaches revelation. The problem that many theologians and teachers run into is that they have a lot of information but often only very little revelation. Some will only operate on an information level and even claim that that is all there is.

All that is is arrogance and dead Christianity. Anything that is not infused with the life-giving power of the Holy Spirit is dead Christianity and run by man's carnal concepts. Our earthly mind is adapted to information, and it understands the concept of information. A person who is conformed to the world only operates according to what that person's earthly mind can fathom. Our spirit, however, is not moved by information but only comes alive through revelation. A spiritual person operates according to their spirit, and only by God's living Spirit can their spirit receive revelation.

The difference between an empowered and powerless Christian life is the difference between living by revelation or information. It is the difference between letting the Holy Spirit renew our mind or holding onto our carnal mind.

"And do not be conformed to this world, but be transformed by the renewing of your mind, that you may prove what is that good and acceptable and perfect will of God" (Romans 12:2, NKJV).

Revelation is knowledge about God, His ways, and His thoughts that goes a lot deeper than any information. Revelation is jam-packed full of grace, faith, and power. It moves us so deeply that in the moment of reception, it immediately births new life deep within us. This life bursts forth from our innermost beings and produces more life around us.

Information, however, cannot produce that life, nor does it come from the inside out but from the outside in. Instead of the innermost desire to please God that can only come by revelation, information is the outside thought that tells us, "You must please God." It is a thought without the power to do, a thought without revelation, and it is a thought of lifeless religion. Without the Holy Spirit giving us revelation, our teachings, our thoughts, and our actions are nothing but a noisy clanging cymbal, but when we are moved by the Spirit, our teachings, our thoughts, and our actions become like a symphony. We flow in the Spirit like being a part of an orchestra that flows in perfect harmony.

We can clearly see this in the disciples' lives. Before the day of Pentecost, they had a pile of information, but they did not truly understand. They had a pile of information, but it did not affect their lives. They did not live empowered lives; they competed, they compared themselves, they were afraid, and they were insecure.

They could not understand the spiritual lessons and revelations that Jesus taught them, and they did not have faith for a spiritual and supernatural life.

After the infilling of the Holy Spirit, however, they walked in power, in love, with faith, with hope, through revelation, and with courage. Peter, who was so afraid that he denied Jesus three times, suddenly became as bold as a lion. He preached the Gospel to the same men who crucified the Lord not long before. Peter, who competed with John before the day of Pentecost, preached together with John after the day of Pentecost. Peter, who did not understand many things that the Lord taught before the day of Pentecost, suddenly taught deep spiritual concepts after the day of Pentecost. What happened? He received the Holy Spirit, and his life and the lives of the other disciples were completely changed. It is the Holy Spirit who empowers us to live this Christian life.

The disciples had to wait until the Holy Spirit was released, just like Jesus had promised them before He ascended. On the day of ascension, Peter still compared himself with John; he was still jealous of John. But after the day of Pentecost, Peter preached together with his rival. This might shock you to hear it, but the church was not born during the days when Jesus was walking on this earth. Nor was the church born on the day of His crucifixion or the day that He rose from the dead. The church was not born on the day of His ascension either, but the church was born on the day of Pentecost. That glorious day when the disciples came out of hiding after being empowered by the Holy Spirit. That day, my friend, was the day Christ's church was born.

After they received the Holy Spirit, Jesus became more real to them than ever before because the Holy Spirit had awakened their spirit. Suddenly, everything that Jesus told them made sense, and His love and power were now upon them. This love and this power enabled them to preach the Gospel in the face of certain death. People often think that it is wrong to give such importance to the

Holy Spirit; they say, "It is all about Jesus." Yes, it is all about Jesus, but without the Holy Spirit, Jesus cannot become real to us. Jesus is in heaven. He is not here on earth, but the Holy Spirit is, and the precious Holy Spirit will never take glory for Himself, but His one mission is to glorify Jesus.

Do you see that by taking out the working of the Holy Spirit, the church can only be dead? The devil knows the power of the Holy Spirit, and he is afraid of His manifestations that glorify Jesus. After all, it was the power of the Holy Spirit that raised Jesus from the dead. The devil knows this, and that is why he has been sending out the spirit of Antichrist to stop the church from having a true and life-changing revelation of Jesus.

How does the spirit of Antichrist prevent people from experiencing Jesus? By undermining, quenching, and attacking the Holy Spirit. He has been very successful in this, as many denominations today reject the fullness of the Holy Spirit and are spiritually dead. They are powerless and lukewarm social clubs that drag people into religion and tradition instead of life and revelation. In the German Empire, the devil used the German church to undermine the Holy Spirit. He could use that church because it was asleep and conformed to this world. It had forgotten the power of the Gospel and the freedom in Christ Jesus.

THE BERLIN DECLARATION OF 1909
(DIE BERLINER ERKLAERUNG)

The Pentecostal movement came to the German Empire in 1907, and there were several revivals that broke out all over the nation. I believe God was pouring out His Spirit to stop the spreading of the spirit of Antichrist in the German Empire. This was a full-on spiritual war in the German Empire, just like what happened in the Roman Empire before. The Holy Spirit was fighting against the spirit of Antichrist. After two years of renewal and revival, the Pentecostal movement had grown. I believe the German Empire could have been turned back into a true Christian nation, but unfortunately, the majority of the German churches made a devastating decision.

You see, the Holy Spirit will never force a person to do anything. He only comes upon those who desire Him and who want to receive Him, just like the disciples wanted Him and were waiting for Him. The devil and the spirit of Antichrist do not ask, nor do they care if a person or nation wants them. They look for open doors and cracks and come in without asking.

The problem with the German church was not just that it had its doors open or that it ignored the importance of the Holy Spirit, but the problem was that the majority of the German church came purposefully against His moving and working among German Christians. Several very influential church leaders wanted to put a stop to the outpouring of the Spirit in Germany. They did not agree with the new life in the German church realm. They did not like the lack of tradition, and they did not believe in the speaking of tongues, prophecies, and the supernatural. Their worldly minds could not see that the Scripture clearly talks about all of these manifestations of the Holy Spirit. Their fleshly approach to Jesus caused them to deny His very Spirit, who was working among them. The influence of the spirit of Antichrist had blinded them, and they could not see the good that was happening in the German Empire. Somehow, they ignored scriptures like this one in the Gospel of Mark.

> And these signs will follow those who believe: In My name they will cast out demons; they will speak with new tongues; they will take up serpents; and if they drink anything deadly, it will by no means hurt them; they will lay hands on the sick, and they will recover.
>
> Mark 16:17 (NKJV)

Their all-too-fleshly minds could not comprehend the things of the Spirit, so those Christian leaders and pastors called a meeting in Berlin in 1909. The purpose of their meeting was to stop the Pentecostal church movement in the German Empire. One of the main leading voices in calling in this meeting was an evangelist named Georg von Viebahn. After a nineteen-hour-long meeting, they came out publicly with the "Berlin Declaration," which officially stated that the Pentecostal movement in which the Holy Spirit moved through speaking in tongues, prophecy, and healings was not from God above but Satan below. The fifty-six pastors and leaders then proceeded to sign this statement and declaration in the capital of the German Empire.

I want you to grasp the gravity of this. No other nation or church has ever written or signed a declaration against the moving of the Holy Spirit ever before or ever since. No other body of Christ in any other nation has publicly and officially distanced themselves in such a way from the Holy Spirit ever before or ever since. It comes as no surprise that the writing and signing of such a declaration by Christian leaders had dire consequences for the entire nation. The Bible says, in Ephesians 4:30 (NKJV), "And do not grieve the Holy Spirit of God, by whom you were sealed for the day of redemption."

Yet that is exactly what the majority of German Christians were led to do. To this very day in Germany, when a person goes to a church other than the traditional Catholic or Protestant church, they are considered by the general public as a member of a cult. I believe that this is one of the lasting rotten fruits of the Berlin Declaration.

The Bible says that by the Holy Spirit, we are sealed for the day of redemption. Can you see the importance of the Holy Spirit? Can you see the catastrophe that a nation or church calls upon itself by grieving the Holy Spirit? The Bible is crystal clear about the importance of the Holy Spirit and His working. There is a line that nobody should cross, and that line is the blasphemy of the Holy Spirit. Jesus Himself warns about this very deed in Matthew 12:31 (NKJV): "Therefore I say to you, every sin and blasphemy will be forgiven men, but the blasphemy against the Spirit will not be forgiven men."

Jesus said that the blasphemy of the Holy Spirit is the only unforgivable sin. But what exactly is blasphemy of the Holy Spirit? It means to show disrespect and a lack of reverence toward Him. It means to insult His holiness and purity. Jesus said it is forgivable if a person blasphemies the Father or the Son but not the Holy Spirit. Does not the very fact that Jesus said this show us the utter importance of the Holy Spirit?

To claim that the moving of the Holy Spirit, his gifts, and his ways are from Satan is in every way blasphemous and is, therefore, an unforgivable sin. To then go a step further and write up and sign an official declaration against the moving of the Holy Spirit in the capital of the German Empire is yet a more grievous form of blasphemy. I find it extremely telling that these Christian leaders were sitting in the capital, Berlin, only a few miles away from the throne of Satan, and instead of writing a declaration against the throne of Satan, they wrote a declaration against the Holy Spirit, the very Spirit who desired to bring life to Germany.

The Holy Spirit is the one that opens our eyes to see spiritual things. He is the one who could have given them a revelation about the throne of Pergamon, but instead, they rejected Him and were listening to the spirit of Antichrist. They could have stopped so much evil from coming into their own nation, but instead, they held onto tradition rather than the Spirit of Liberty.

"Making the word of God of no effect through your tradition which you have handed down. And many such things you do" (Mark 7:13, NKJV).

Now, you may wonder and ask, "How is it that the spirit of Antichrist was stronger than the Holy Spirit in the German Empire?"

The reason why the spirit of Antichrist prevailed in the German Empire is because this declaration came from the German church. This is a spiritual principle that many Christians need to understand. The government of a nation does not direct society; it is the church that directs society. The society of a nation is always a reflection of the church. It is the church's call and responsibility to affect the society around it.

In nations like China, where the church is heavily persecuted, this may take decades, but just like in China, the true church will always affect society, even in the highest form of government. God gave the church much power over darkness and principalities. The government has no power in such realms. Governments may decide to fight a war in the natural world, but we Christians fight wars in the spiritual realm, and while we do not wrestle with flesh and blood, we believers are not without the weapons of faith, praise, worship, and the Word of God that is sharper than a two-edged sword. Many Christians, however, do not use their weapons.

The reason why the spirit of Antichrist could take hold of an entire nation like the German Empire was because the German church not only disregarded its spiritual weapons but also empowered the spirit of Antichrist. It did this by rejecting the church's General, the Holy Spirit, who would have enabled the church to wield its spiritual weapons. Without Him, the church has no faith, no truth in worship, and no revelation power in the scriptures.

The declaration was written in 1909, and within five years, the First World War began. The German Empire was not just one nation among other nations in World War I, but it became the driving force in this war when it declared war on Russia and France and invaded the neutral nation of Belgium. After four years of fighting, twenty million people were dead, of which ten million were civilians.

After the German Empire lost the war, the other nations wanted to never see it rise up again. The nations who had won the war made the decision that the German Empire would have to pay extremely high reparations. The punishment that the German Empire received was so harsh that economists at the time said it would bring economic collapse to the entire European continent. To this day, historians believe that the punishment was over the top and actually triggered great resentment and bitterness in the German people. They believe that this resentment in the German people prepared a perfect platform for Adolf Hitler to rise to power.

While all of that might be true, I see something deeper in the harsh reparations fines that the German Empire received. I see it as God's judgment. Judgment for a nation that had not only opened its doors to the spirit of Antichrist and walked away from God and His principles but also rejected the Holy Spirit. I call it God's judgment because the German Empire did not fight in World War I alone but had allies like Hungary-Austria, Bulgaria, and the Ottoman Empire. Yet the German Empire was made the sole aggressor of World War I and the only nation that received penalties for fighting that war.

The Treaty of Versailles, in which the reparations amount was set to thirty-three billion US dollars, was signed only ten years after the blasphemous Berlin Declaration was signed. Judgment upon a person or nation only comes if the person or nation is guilty. I believe that the nations in charge of the Treaty of Versailles were used by God to judge the German Empire. The name of the clause that they used to enforce punishment upon the German Empire suited the spiritual judgment given. They named it "The War Guilt Clause."

The shame, the guilt, and the high reparations, however, were not the end of the suffering of Germany. The spirit of Antichrist still had a firm grip on Germany, and his work was not yet done. If you give the devil a little finger, he will always take the whole hand.

HITLER AND THE THRONE OF SATAN

In the aftermath of World War I, the German Empire fell apart, and Germany turned into a republic. Communism was on the rise, and so was nationalism. Everyone knows what happened next. Adolf Hitler came on the scene. In 1933, only twenty-four years after the Berlin Declaration was written, Adolf Hitler became the new chancellor of Germany. In Adolf Hitler, the spirit of Antichrist found a new vessel whom he would use. A person does not have to look very hard to recognize the evil that came out of Hitler. His hate for the Jewish people and his hate for the church became clearer and clearer throughout his rule.

This is when history almost gets bizarre. It is shocking how openly the devil plays his cards, but yet so many at that time and even to this day do not see it. In the years in which Hitler came to power, he and his Nazi henchmen would conduct large rallies in the city of Nuremberg. These rallies were strategically planned and caused a frenzy among the Germans. The spirit of Antichrist laid so heavily upon Hitler that the crowds literally worshiped him. They loved Hitler, and in those rallies, he appeared to the masses like a god. The scene around him was created to be mystical, and he would appear out of the pitch-black surroundings with the use of torches and flood lights. The very stage that Hitler spoke from was no ordinary stage but happened to be an exact replica of the throne of Satan from the Pergamon Museum. From this very altar of Satan, Hitler addressed the German masses and won their hearts to follow him wherever he would lead. From this altar, he spoke against the Jews and, with many deceptive words, prepared the people's hearts for yet another war and the Holocaust.

THE SPIRIT OF THE ANTICHRIST IN HITLER'S GERMANY

The spirit of Antichrist's target is to defame Jesus and everything and everyone that is connected to Him. The spirit of Antichrist goes after Christians and not Jews, but this spirit obviously comes from the devil, and the devil hates anything that God loves. The spirit of Antichrist is not on his own mission separate from the devil's. This spirit was sent by the devil, who seized the opportunity to not only spread the spirit of Antichrist in Germany but also to go after God's own people, the Jews. Six million Jews were slaughtered and treated worse than animals throughout Hitler's reign.

It is impossible to fathom that normal people could cause such evil to another race. What happened to the Jews in the concentration camps shocked the entire world. For many years, the public's opinion was that most Germans during Hitler's rule did not know about the concentration camps and what happened in them; however, recent studies by several renowned historians show quite the opposite. After extensive research and the studying of newspaper articles from that time period, historians came out with a chilling conclusion: most Germans knew about the Holocaust and supported the removal of the Jewish people.

The question arises: how could a human being support such evil? Only a spirit could cause people to do such evil. Only a spirit can take hold of an entire nation or group of people and make them behave in this manner. The Antichrist's spirit had been working for many years in the German lands; unchecked and not confronted by the German church, he was able to twist the hearts of many.

Hitler, in many ways, gives us a picture of what the final Antichrist might look like. He was the perfect candidate for the spirit of Antichrist. He was very charismatic and a very talented speaker. He promised the people work and freedom, and most importantly, he gave the Germans back their pride after the shame that came upon them from the loss of World War I. If the German people had received the Holy Spirit and found in Him the counsel, comfort, love, and truth that He brings, they would not have been receptive to the spirit of Antichrist in Adolf Hitler. But their eyes were closed, and so it is with many people today. Things are happening before our eyes but many don't see. At the end of his life, Hitler committed suicide, just like Emperor Nero. Once the spirit of Antichrist was done using his earthly vessels, there was nothing left in them that desired life.

A look at the people who surrounded Hitler shows us the working of the spirit of Antichrist even more. One of these men was Adolf Eichmann, who made it his life's mission to murder Jews. Men who worked for Eichmann described him as having no human feelings toward the Jews. He was ice-cold and had no morals. Besides Adolf Eichmann, there were many other men who were invested in killing Jews. Two of them were Josef Mengele and Heinrich Himmler. Just like Hitler, Mengele and Himmler had strong ties to the occult. In the concentration camps, Josef Mengele would conduct medical and surgical experiments on the Jews. These were so barbaric that even unbelieving historians would describe his experiments later on as simply satanic. Himmler's mission was also satanic, as he was actually the one who came up with the idea for the Holocaust. His mission was not only to kill all the Jews but to literally de-Christianize the entire country of Germany and for the nation to return to its former Germanic paganism.

HAS GOD FORSAKEN GERMANY?

After revealing Germany's chilling spiritual history, these questions might arise: "Has God forsaken Germany because of its past?" or "Is Germany's future doomed?" The answer to both questions is no. God has not forsaken Germany, nor is its future doomed. There are many sincere and devoted Christians in Germany today who love Jesus and who are spreading the good news of Him all over the country. Just the other day, I saw a video of a powerful revival in the streets of Hamburg. I believe that no matter how dark Germany's past or even current state is, God still wants His kingdom to be built in that nation, and God still has good plans for the people. To effectively proclaim the good news and to successfully build

God's kingdom, however, I believe the church must not ignore the dark spiritual past of Germany. I do not believe that the German church must dwell on it or be imprisoned by it but rather must use the knowledge of the reasons for this dark past to peel back the darkness in that land. There were times in the Old Testament when Israel was infested by idolatry and witchcraft, but the works of faithful men and women pierced through that great darkness. These loyal ministers reaffirmed Israel's great destiny, and eras of great glory followed. If I can give a word to my Christian brothers and sisters in Germany, it is this: Do not give up and do not back down. For your heavenly Father will show Himself strong on your behalf. Preach the full Gospel in the full power of the Spirit and build God's kingdom one soul at a time.

"For the eyes of the LORD run to and fro throughout the whole earth, to show Himself strong on behalf of those whose heart is loyal to Him" (2 Chronicles 16:9, NKJV).

— CHAPTER 9: —
THE LEOPARD AND THE SPIRIT OF THE ANTICHRIST

As I wrote in the previous chapter, Communism came into existence in the German Empire in the nineteenth century. Right after Karl Marx and Friedrich Engels wrote *The Communist Manifesto*, the Communist ideology started to spread across Europe. While Communist ideas spread rather fast, it took almost seventy years after the manifesto was released for Communism to take hold of an entire nation. Long after Marx's and Engel's death, a young man named Vladimir Lenin embraced this demonic ideology and advocated for it like no one else before him.

Vladimir Lenin was born in the Russian Empire on April 22, 1870. At the age of fifteen, after his father's death, Lenin denounced his faith in God. Just like Marx and Engels, he became a staunch atheist. In his late teen years, he read Karl Marx's book *Capital* and started to be interested in Marx's ideology. By 1889, at the age of nineteen, Lenin had fully embraced Communism. Shortly after, he himself translated Karl Marx's and Friedrich Engels' Communist Manifesto in its entirety into Russian.

This evil ideology needed a carrier, an advocate, and a pioneer. Its intended purpose was much more than just a collection of new thoughts and theories. The devil designed it to be lived out and to spread atheism across the globe. The spirit of Antichrist desperately needed someone to put it into action, and Lenin became that someone. Over the coming years, Lenin became a lead figure in the Marxist movement in Russia, where he openly spread Marxist ideas. He had connections with fellow Marxists all over Europe, and his one goal was to establish Communism. He wanted to overthrow the rule of the czar in Russia; he wanted to see the end of capitalism, monarchy, and the aristocracy. In order to turn the Russian Empire into a Communist nation, Lenin believed that a Communist revolution was needed. He did not just want to see his native land, Russia, turn Communist, but he wanted to see a revolution that would spread all across Europe and even further.

After imprisonment and years of struggle, Lenin finally succeeded in turning the Russian Empire into a Communist nation when he led the famous October Revolution in October 1917. In this revolution, Lenin and his Bolshevik party overthrew the monarchy and, with it, the government of the nobles. Right after the revolution, a civil war broke out, and the country fell into anarchy. The Bolsheviks, under Lenin, fought a group of allies that included monarchists, democratic socialists, and capitalists. Lenin's side was called the Red Army, and the opposing side was called the White Army. The Russian Civil War cost ten million lives, and in the end, the Bolsheviks under Lenin won that war.

For the first time in history, an entire nation was now under the Communist ideology. This was not just any nation, but the spirit of Antichrist had succeeded in turning the biggest nation on earth into a Communist nation. Under the leadership of Lenin and the Bolshevik party, all religions, especially Christianity, were under systematic attack. Persecution began from the very moment that they began to rule. This move to blot out religion was unparalleled to anything prior in the history of this world. In Lenin's eyes, Christianity was a sickness. He wrote in one of his writings,

> Religion is the opium of the people: this saying of Marx is the cornerstone of the entire ideology of Marxism about religion. All modern religions and churches, all and of every kind of religious organizations are always considered by Marxism as the organs of bourgeois reaction, used for the protection of the exploitation and the stupefaction of the working class.[4]

The Communist government enforced a cleansing of anything referring to religion. This indeed meant every religion, but it is important to state that Russia was not a nation with all kinds of religions. No, Russia was a Christian nation. Before Communism, Orthodox Christianity was the state religion. The same was true for the German Empire when Marx and Engels wrote their book. At that time, the German Empire was, on paper, a Christian nation. Is Communism against every religion? Technically, yes, but in truth, its main enemy is Christianity. History shows clearly that Communist leaders have predominantly fought Christians. Have you ever heard of a massive Communist revolution in a Muslim nation or a Hindu nation?

If a person looks at the three most well-known Communist revolutions in which entire nations turned to Communism, the picture becomes very clear. In Russia, a Christian nation, the Christians were predominately persecuted. In Cuba, a Christian nation that turned Communist, the Christians were predominately persecuted. In China, a nation in which the Christian church was growing rapidly, the Communist party persecuted the Christians most severely. All three of the Communist nations just mentioned ultimately turned against the Christian church more than any other religion.

When Lenin took over Russia, the vast majority of Russians be-

---

4   Lenin Collected Works (Progress Publishers, 1973).

lieved in God, but the Communists wanted to delete God from people's hearts and minds. Churches and monasteries were destroyed, priests and clergy were assassinated, and leading Christian voices were silenced and sent to work camps. Children in school no longer heard about God because the Communists took any reference to God out of the curriculum. The new state religion under Lenin was atheism. It is vital for us to understand that atheism is not a byproduct of Communism but the main pillar.

When a nation or a government turns against God in such a way, the consequences are often devastating. Even at the very beginning of Lenin's rule, the population of Russia started to suffer unimaginably. Not just because of the horror of the civil war but also because severe famine hit, causing hardship and many deaths. Severe droughts hit the land, and the mismanagement of the country by Lenin's government resulted in the death of millions of people. The famine was so severe that the more poor Russian people turned to cannibalism to survive. People were murdered so that their bodies could be consumed. Dead people were dug up and eaten. Even within families, there was cannibalism; parents would kill and eat their children, and siblings would eat one another. All over Russia, there were black market trades in human flesh and body parts. Human meat was even ground up so that it was visually not distinguishable.

Similarly to Karl Marx, Lenin suffered from a terrible illness, continuous headaches, and insomnia. He also suffered from hyperacusis, which is an over-sensitivity to noise to such a degree that it brings severe fear and pain to the person who suffers from it. He considered suicide and even asked Josef Stalin at one point to bring him potassium cyanide so that he could kill himself. Lenin had three strokes and died at the age of fifty-three from an incurable blood vessel disease.

Now that the stage was set for Communism, with Russia being its forerunner, other nations under the rule of evil leaders all over the world followed Russia's example. History has not forgotten any of these evil Communist rulers, and history shows us that all these Communist leaders turned against Christianity. A guess as to who was behind all this? The spirit of Antichrist was, and for many years, it successfully pushed down the Gospel in many parts of the world. It was after Lenin, in the era of the third beast, that Communism started to truly spread all over the world. Over the next few pages, I will highlight some of the men who were used by the spirit of Antichrist during the era of the third beast.

STALIN

Joseph Stalin was born in 1878 and was Lenin's successor, ruling for thirty years until his death in 1953. At the age of ten, he attended an Orthodox Christian school, and by the age of sixteen, he became a trainee priest at an Orthodox theological seminary. But just like Lenin, he became an atheist in his late teen years. Stalin was also a strong anti-Semite, and many Jews were murdered or sent to labor camps by him. During his purge, Stalin ordered the shooting of thousands of priests, pastors, and ministers. He hated everything about Christianity—so much so that he pushed other Communist leaders, like Kim Il Sung of North Korea, to fully eradicate Christianity. Stalin was a paranoid and ruthless leader. He forced his form of Communism without mercy. No matter how many lives it would cost, Stalin was committed to seeing it through. The death toll caused by this man was far more than Hitler's, and the weight of the deaths of millions of people was evident in his life. The terror that he imposed on the people through his absolute dictatorship scared even his closest friends. He was unpredictable and absolutely unbalanced. He said about himself that he had a heart of stone.

Everything about him, from his personal life to his rulership and even his death, speaks about the working of the spirit of Antichrist. His own daughter was traumatized for the rest of her life by witnessing his death. Stalin had a severe stroke, and just before he died, he raised his hand and spoke forth inaudible words. In his face was hate and menace. She said it was like he was speaking forth a curse over someone or something and then died. Before he died, his doctors were paralyzed with fear and would not help because they were too afraid of him. His two decades of terror prevented him from receiving medical help when he needed it. Even his own funeral resulted in more deaths when hundreds of people trampled each other at the funeral proceedings. I do not take pleasure in writing down all the terrible details of these evil men, but my reason for doing it is to show you the handwriting of the spirit of Antichrist. He will stop at nothing to attempt to destroy Christianity and Christian lives. Stalin was not the first nor the last man that was used by this spirit.

MAO ZEDONG

Born in China, Mao accepted the Communist ideology while going to university in Peking. His conversion to Communism happened after exposing himself for years to the works of Western political philosophers like Adam Smith, Montesquieu, and Jean-Jacques Rousseau. Their writings prepared the way for Mao to accept the Marxist ideology, as Western philosophy has the same author as Communism: the spirit of Antichrist. Mao was the key figure in leading China into becoming a Communist nation. After years of bloody civil wars, protests, and revolutions, Mao declared the People's Republic of China on October 1, 1949. His nation was both to be a Communist and atheist state.

As a dictator, he ruled over the people with absolute terror. The control that the Chinese people were under is hard to put into words. Unlike Stalin, Mao's henchmen tortured, humiliated, and executed people in public for everyone to watch. His strategy was even darker as he succeeded in getting the Chinese people involved in the punishments. The people spied on each other and betrayed each other to the Chinese government. Friends betrayed friends, kids betrayed parents, and parents betrayed kids. To own books was a crime, and to own a Bible was the worst. The only book people were allowed to own was a collection of the Communist writings of Mao himself. His economic and social reforms and his cultural revolution killed millions and millions of innocent people.

During the Cultural Revolution, the government turned with vigor against all the Christians in China. A specific plan was made by the government to fully eradicate Christianity. While countless Christians and churches suffered terribly, just like the Roman government under Nero, the Chinese government was unable to stop Christianity from spreading. At the time of Mao's death in 1979, he was responsible for between forty to eighty million deaths. It is important to state that these are peacetime deaths. Meaning they were not the result of any war but simply of Mao's rule over his own people. Executions, famines, and imprisonment caused these deaths. For what goal, you may wonder? To establish a Communist, anti-Christian China and to follow the call of the spirit of Antichrist.

CHE GUEVARA

Che Guevara was born in Argentina in 1928. He was what I would call the missionary of Communism. He traveled all over the world and attempted to establish Communism in several struggling third-world countries. He was a Communist revolutionary, guerrilla leader, and author. He had a deep hatred for anything peaceful, and he wanted to see war and death for the cause of Communism. He is supposed to once have said, *"In fact, if Christ himself stood in my way, I, like Nietzsche, would not hesitate to squish him like a worm."*

Che Guevara influenced the world of Communism greatly, perhaps even more after his death than when he was alive. His portrait became an international symbol of rebellion and revolution and is still used by ignorant people today. *Time* magazine called him one of the most influential people of the twentieth century.

FIDEL CASTRO

Fidel Castro was born in Cuba in 1926. He embraced the Communist ideology while going to the University of Havana. After adopting the ideology and being fueled by revolutionary thoughts, he attempted to remove Cuba's prime minister, Fulgencio Batista, with the help of his revolutionary friends. The attempt failed, and many of Castro's friends died during the attack or were later executed. Castro himself went to prison to only serve a fraction of his prison sentence. Once he came out of prison, he left Cuba and went to Mexico, where he formed a group of revolutionaries, which included Che Guevara. With this group, he started a guerrilla war against Batista and his regime. This time, he succeeded and became Cuba's prime minister and military leader in 1959.

Upon Castro's power grab, Cuba became the first Communist nation in the Western world. Cuba was now led by a Communist party, of which Castro was the leader. His dictatorship lasted from 1959 to 2008, almost sixty years. He also empowered and supported other Communist regimes in nations like Nicaragua, Grenada, and Chile. His vision, like Lenin's, was to transform the world into a Communist world.

After establishing strong connections with the Soviet Union, Castro permitted the Soviets to move nuclear weapons to Cuba in order to threaten the United States during the Cold War. This was a moment in which the whole world was holding its breath. Two forces were one button push away from bringing utter destruction upon the entire world.

The Cuban population suffered terribly under his regime. The abuse of freedom and human rights was very severe. With the implantation of Communism, the economy went downhill, and poverty grew all over Cuba. Castro was responsible for the deaths of thousands of Cubans. Even his own daughter fled the country and applied for asylum in the United States in 1993. Like all true Communist leaders, Castro hated Christianity. Since Cuba was a predominantly Christian nation, this called for the persecution of many Catholic Christians. Churches were closed, Christmas was banned, and many priests and pastors were imprisoned. Under Castro's Communist regime, Cuba became an atheist nation. To this day, you can see the scars from the destructive years of Communism.

THE SPIRIT OF THE ANTICHRIST IN THE WESTERN WORLD

While the rest of the world was being bombarded with Communism, Islam, and other Eastern religions, the spirit of Antichrist came up with a different tactic in the Western world. There were several course-altering movements since the end of World War II that were fueled by this destructive spirit.

The Hippie Movement

Often, when we think about hippies, we have a certain picture in our heads. We immediately think of peaceful, gentle, and easy-going people. A person could think, "What is the harm in that?" While I do believe that peace and gentleness are indeed good Christian virtues, they are not the true virtues behind the hippie movement. On the outside, many worldly things look attractive, but on the inside, they often are the opposite.

The hippie movement was not an accidental occurrence but strategically planned by the kingdom of darkness. You might be surprised to hear this, but I believe the spirit of Antichrist was also the instigator of this movement. Sixty years later, we still see the moral decline that this movement has brought upon the Western world.

Let me explain.

Did you know that the hippie movement was officially named a *counterculture* movement? This term was not just used by people who opposed this movement, but it was also used by its partisans. As the word implies, counterculture describes a cultural movement that goes against the current culture of a nation or group of people. Knowing what a counterculture movement is and knowing that the hippie movement indeed had such an agenda, we must ask the following question: what was the culture of the United States in the 1960s that the hippie movement came against?

The answer is crystal clear: a Christian culture.

Isn't it interesting that the hippie movement did not occur in Communist Russia, China, or in a Muslim or Buddhist nation? Is it just a coincidence that the hippie movement only befell Western countries? Of course not. This was a purposeful and strategic attack.

No other country was hit harder by this movement than America because, at the time, no other nation identified as strongly with Christian values. If we look at America today, we still see Christian values, but if you would ask your parents or grandparents about how society was back then, you would hear about how much more Christian America was back then.

The hippie movement hit America in the 1960s and was accompanied by popular music, fashion, television, and the arts. This was not an accident but was cunningly crafted by the spirit of Antichrist so that being a hippie would be appealing to young people in order to pull them away from God. It was also no coincidence that this hippie movement started while America was in the middle of fighting Communism, another trickery of the spirit of Antichrist.

People often say that the Vietnam War was senseless, and many have made the Vietnam War a shameful war. While I in no way promote war or the killing of people, I would like to point something out. When you look at this war with natural eyes, most people would agree that it was a senseless war. What if we look at this war with spiritual eyes? Once again, I am not promoting war, but what I see in the Vietnam War is that the leader of the Christian world, America, was fighting against the spirit of Antichrist that was expressing itself through Communism. For decades, the United States of America, along with its Christian allies, fought the spread of the Communist ideology. Then, suddenly, within America and the Western world, a counterculture hippie movement started, which protested effectively against this very war. Can you see what was happening? People say this war was only started for economic reasons, but could it be that there was more going on? Something deeper? Something spiritual?

The hippie movement's true face was hiding behind the appealing new music, the free arts, and the provocative fashion styles. At the core of this movement was an anti-Christian ideology that shook an entire generation. The culture of the hippie movement was filled with Eastern philosophy and Eastern religion that led many young people into bondage. It was all about peace and love, they proclaimed, but the Prince of Peace and the true Lover of our souls was not welcome. Jesus' teaching about love and peace was tolerated, but in the same breath, His truth and His way to repentance and freedom from sin were rejected. Both of my parents were victims of the hippie movement, and through it, both were sucked into drugs and Eastern religion. It was only by the grace of God and through the Jesus People movement that both of them were found by Jesus and started to follow Him.

Many people believe that the hippie movement started in America, but that is not accurate. It started somewhere else, a place where many other dark movements originated from—Germany.

After the German Empire was founded and right around the time when the first pieces of the throne of Satan were brought to Berlin, the first hippie youth movement started in the German Empire. These hippies are also called the "proto-hippies." This new countercultural movement consisted of thousands of young people who listened to German folk music, dressed creatively, and promoted hiking and the outdoors, but that was not all. These first German hippies were very connected to the works of Nietzsche and Goethe, the two German authors who had strong ties to the demonic and the Freemason culture. The proto-hippies publicly expressed their desire to see the German Empire leave its Christian and urbanizing culture and go back to its pagan culture from the past. In the early twentieth century, this culture was then brought to the United States by Germans who immigrated to California. Some of these spiritual connections and avenues are mind-boggling, and the reality of those things should certainly open our eyes as believers. Let us not perish for lack of knowledge, but let us embrace the guidance of the Holy Spirit, who opens our eyes.

Even though the hippie movement did not last long, dwindling rather quickly in the mid-1970s, it still had a huge effect on America and the rest of the world. I believe that the spirit of Antichrist never intended to turn every American into a hippie but that this movement's purpose was to break the protective walls of the Christian culture in this nation.

The hippie movement was the dam breaker. It released a flood wave of filth all over America. With the hippie movement came strong perversion, and sexual sin crept deeply into American society. These years are known as the sexual revolution. Hippies promoted open relationships and encouraged people to experiment with sex. This movement promoted homosexuality, public nudity, and group sex. The spirit of Antichrist was extremely successful, as the door that was opened in the 1960s has never been closed again in the United States. Over the years, more and more filth came through this door, and today, our generation is bombarded with sexual junk day in and day out. Once a dam is broken, the force of water pushing through makes it nearly impossible to repair the dam. Today we are not only witnessing homosexuality, open relationships, and adultery, but we are witnessing transgenderism, pedophilia, and pornography that is at everyone's fingertips.

God designed sex, and there is nothing evil about sex when practiced in a marriage covenant between a man and a woman. It is a beautiful act of intimacy between a man and a woman that makes them become one flesh. It was beautifully and lovingly designed by our heavenly Father. The spirit of Antichrist undermined God's perfect design during the hippie movement and seared the conscience of many people in the Western world.

Feminism

What started in the Western world with the hippies has been made worse in today's society. Through this counterculture movement, the spirit of Antichrist opened the doors for many other sub-movements that, at their very core, also go against God's design. The spirit of Antichrist understands that in order to turn people from God, to create a secular, godless culture, it must undermine God's order first. God's order will always bring protection for everyone under it. But when His order is compromised, protection and safety are nowhere to be found. In the same breath as the hippie movement, the feminist movement was launched in the United States and the Western world, leading women to fight against the traditional roles of their sex and working to make women equal to men in all areas of life.

Even many Christians have been subconsciously influenced by this movement mainly because they mistake *position* with *value*. Feminists believe that women should have the same responsibilities as men. While feminists are right about the fact that women are as *valuable* as men, they are absolutely wrong about the fact that women should have the same responsibilities. A woman was created by God to be a woman, and a man was created to be a man. Cultural changes cannot alter the written Word of God. If culture indeed can alternate the Bible, then the Bible becomes instantly ineffective. Just because culture and society are changing does not give us Christians the right to change or ignore God's Word and order. The truths of the Bible are timeless; they stand resolute for all generations to come.

We read in the Bible that the man is the head of the house and the head of the wife. His responsibility is to love his wife like Christ loves the church. Jesus is asking every husband and father to lay down his life for his wife and his children. That is not optional, but that is the responsibility of the husband and father. This responsibility does not make the husband more valuable than the woman. That, however, is exactly what the devil has whispered into many women's ears through the feminist movement.

A woman was designed to be a helpmate to her husband. Unfortunately, many people get angry when they hear that because they do not understand the value of a helper. In the beginning, God saw that it was not good for a man to be alone. He saw that the man needed a woman. Does not the very thought that man could not live a fulfilled life without the woman make women utterly valuable? God made the woman from the rib of the man. As I wrote earlier in this book, the rib bone is the only bone that can regrow and regenerate. That, by the way, is the power of a godly wife. When the husband comes home defeated, discouraged, and ready to give up, his wife has the extraordinary power to rebuild him with encouragement, love, and nurturing. The rib bones are also the very bones in the human body that protect the vital organs and help us to walk upright. Once again, that is exactly the calling of the wife. She protects the man's heart through respect and encouragement, and she helps him to fulfill his purpose and makes him walk upright.

A woman, on the other hand, is looking for affection. It is affection that makes her feel loved and valuable. Every woman has a deep desire inside of her to be precious to her husband and her father. If the husband or father neglects to affirm this God-given desire of the woman, the woman will sense no value. A woman who senses no value from her husband or father will then often attempt to gain value, taking on unnatural responsibilities. The key to destroying the feminist movement is found in God's unchangeable quest for the man: men must love their wives and daughters like Christ loves the church. A husband who lays down his life for his wife says, "You are valuable, and you are worth it by simply being who you are."

Feminism does not promote that way of thinking and lies to women. The spirit of Antichrist tells them that they have to achieve big things for them to gain value. God and a godly husband, on the other hand, say, "You do not have to achieve big things; you do not have to perform in order to convince me to lay my life down for you. You are already valuable."

All that being said, can a woman do great things for God, her nation, or her family? Absolutely, the motivation, however, is what matters. Is it to gain value, or is it to fulfill God's call on her life? If she is called by God like Queen Esther or Deborah, she must fulfill that call, and God will use her to glorify His Son Jesus. God's call, however, never changes His own order. Both Esther and Deborah were submitted to men. Esther was submitted to Mordecai and the king, and Deborah was submitted to her own husband. If you are a Christian woman and you are reading this, be encouraged and answer God's call with all your strength and fervency. Do not be timid in this pursuit; don't just succumb to the pressures of society by leaving the protection of God's perfect order.

Feminism promises women freedom by not submitting to God's order, but in reality, they are getting sucked into bondage. It is only in God's will that all of us are truly free. Outside of His will and order, we become slaves to sin. The spirit of Antichrist knows God's design. He knows the protection that a husband will bring to his wife and children. He knows that the husband and father are the spiritual leaders of the family, so by removing the husband as a safeguard, the devil has access to the wife and kids. A house that is divided against itself cannot stand. A woman who is convinced of the lies of feminism will bring her house to fall. A man who is delinquent and will not stand as a spiritual leader in the house will cause the destruction of his wife and kids. Can you see how this movement has influenced the culture of America, the Western world, and even the church?

God needs fiery women evangelists, prophetesses, and preachers. God needs fiery mothers, businesswomen, and prayer warriors. Find the One who calls you, then find your calling. Once found, remain in His order and build His kingdom in boldness and love!

Abortion

Feminism came with the hippie movement, and through feminism, one of the darkest atrocities in the history of the world began: abortion. In the 1970s, abortion was made legal, and since then, millions of innocent and helpless babies have been killed in the wombs of women. The very place that should provide safety, nurture, and the first feeling of love, the mother's womb, became a crime scene and a place of murder. The baby in the womb, who is so dependent on the mother's care, love, and protection, is betrayed before it can even see the light of this world. Betrayed by the very person who was supposed to love that baby. How can a woman commit such a heartless crime? How can a woman kill her own child? Only a spirit could cause such deception and hatred against an innocent being. Only the spirit of Antichrist that is sent by the one who kills, steals, and destroys could make a woman believe that she is doing the right thing.

Women believe, by killing their own babies, that they stand up for their right to have a choice. The truth is that they do have a choice, but their choice cannot be murder. Their choice is to either abstain from sex or prevent conception with many different products. Once conception happens and life has come forth, there is no more choice to go back. Can you see the root of feminism in abortion? Abortion is based on the lie that a woman can have sex without carrying the responsibility of it. The devil, indeed, is a master deceiver and liar. An entire culture has been fooled by his wicked schemes. I know there are rare cases of women who are raped and then become pregnant. Those are just terrible circumstances, and all of our hearts and prayers should go out to those who experience this atrocious crime. We must pray for them and help them in any way. Yet even in those dark circumstances, the question must be asked: "Why should an innocent baby pay for the crime by being aborted?" It wasn't the baby's choice! Please consider its precious life.

> Many people are concerned with children of India, with the children of Africa where quite a few die of hunger, and so on. Many people are also concerned about the violence in this great country of the United States. These concerns are very good. But often these same people are not concerned with the millions being killed by the deliberate decision of their own mothers. And this is the greatest destroyer of peace today—abortion which brings people to such blindness.
>
> Mother Teresa (National Prayer Breakfast, 1994)

The spirit of Antichrist has successfully used this movement to destroy the sanctity of life in the Western world. If a society can kill its own in the wombs and feel good about that, then this society is not influenced by the Spirit of the living God but by the spirit of Antichrist.

"These six things the Lord hates, Yes, seven are an abomination to Him: A proud look, A lying tongue, Hands that shed innocent blood" (Proverbs 6:16–17, NKJV).

God hates the shedding of innocent blood, and He will hold all of us accountable. You may not be an abortion doctor, and you may not be a woman who has had an abortion, but let me ask you: have you voted for a party that stands for abortion? Your vote matters, and God will not forget the votes that we cast. Right now, in America, it could not be clearer; we have one side that stands for abortion and another side that stands against it. Who will you vote for? No financial benefit or other stance that a party holds will justify your vote for them if it will bring death upon the unborn.

Please: If you have committed sin by having an abortion, supported abortion in any way, or are a doctor or politician who was or is involved in abortions, I want to tell you it is not too late. Repent and turn from your ways and throw yourself at the foot of the cross of Jesus. Confess your sin and ask the Prince of Peace for forgiveness.

PART III: THE FOURTH BEAST

— CHAPTER 10: —
INTRODUCTION INTO THE FOURTH BEAST

GOD AND HIS PROPHETS

To attempt to understand the fourth beast, we must go through the scriptures systematically and diligently. We also must answer two important questions in this chapter:

1. Is Daniel's vision of the fourth beast for us?

2. Do we live in the end times?

The truth is that a person could come up with many exciting theories about this beast and probably make them sound very appealing and plausible. I myself have no interest in coming up with any theories as I believe that theories about this beast will not produce much fruit. A person cannot just press into God's mysteries and prophecies without Him revealing them by His Spirit to that person first. To come up with theories, however, is exactly that. It is the pressing into heavenly things without the influence of His Spirit.

Did you know that God does nothing unless He reveals it to His prophets first? In Amos 3:7 (NKJV), we find this amazing truth:

"Surely the Lord God does nothing, Unless He reveals His secret to His servants the prophets."

Is that not amazing? One of God's principles is to do nothing without notifying His prophets and giving them an understanding of what He is doing. Think about this: every biblical prophecy was recorded for God's people to understand what He is doing. Otherwise, why did He give these prophecies and visions in the first place? What a faithful God we serve. He wants us to understand the times we are in, and He wants us to know what He is doing.

While we will never understand everything He is doing, He has revealed many important past and future events through biblical prophecy, and He will continue to reveal things to His people through present prophecy.

While I do not claim to be a prophet, the reason why I am writing about the four beasts is because I believe that the Lord has given me an understanding of Daniel's vision that is relevant to God's people today. I also believe that there are other people and prophets to whom God will reveal, or already has revealed, insights into Daniel's vision. I also want for you, the reader, to understand that this chapter is not a "Thus says the Lord" chapter. I am simply giving you some insight that I believe the Holy Spirit has revealed to me. I must also say that my understanding of this fourth beast is not unlimited; I felt called to only write down the things that I do understand about this beast.

THE BEAST'S SIGNIFICANCE

> After this I saw in the night visions, and behold, a fourth beast, dreadful and terrible, exceedingly strong. It had huge iron teeth; it was devouring, breaking in pieces, and trampling the residue with its feet. It was different from all the beasts that were before it, and it had ten horns. I was considering the

> horns, and there was another horn, a little one, coming up among them, before whom three of the first horns were plucked out by the roots. And there, in this horn, were eyes like the eyes of a man, and a mouth speaking pompous words.
>
> Daniel 7:7–8 (NKJV)

The fourth beast is very significant. Daniel himself continues referring to this beast while almost ignoring the other beasts. Daniel repeatedly comments on its power and how different it is, while he is drawn to understand more about it.

"After this I saw in the night visions, and behold, a fourth beast, dreadful and terrible, exceedingly strong" (Daniel 7:7, NKJV).

"Then I wished to know the truth about the fourth beast, which was different from all the others" (Daniel 7:19, NKJV).

Daniel relentlessly pressed in to grasp more about the fourth beast. After all that pressing in, it appears that an angel gives him a deeper interpretation of the fourth beast. Here is the extra interpretation that Daniel receives.

> Thus he said: "The fourth beast shall be a fourth kingdom on earth, which shall be different from all other kingdoms, and shall devour the whole earth, trample it and break it in pieces. The ten horns are ten kings who shall arise from this kingdom. And another shall rise after them; He shall be different from the first ones, and shall subdue three kings. He shall speak pompous words against the Most High, shall persecute the saints of the Most High, and shall intend to change times and law. Then the saints shall be given into his hand for a time and times and half a time.

"But the court shall be seated, and they shall take away his dominion, To consume and destroy it forever. Then the kingdom and dominion, and the greatness of the kingdoms under the whole heaven, shall be given to the people, the saints of the Most High. His kingdom is an everlasting kingdom, and all dominions shall serve and obey Him."

Daniel 7:23–27 (NKJV)

The interpretation that he received certainly gave Daniel some answers, but yet it appears that this interpretation also gave Daniel more questions. I say this because at the end of his account, he says, "This is the end of the account. As for me, Daniel, my thoughts greatly troubled me, and my countenance changed; but I kept the matter in my heart" (Daniel 7:28, NKJV).

Would a person be affected by receiving such a powerful vision? Absolutely yes! Reading it in the context, however, shows strong emotion on Daniel's end. He said, *"My thoughts greatly troubled me."* To me, that sounds like a person who is still trying to understand this vision and the implications of it.

Another key remark that leads me to believe that Daniel did not fully understand this vision is found earlier in Daniel 7:15 (NKJV): "I, Daniel, was grieved in my spirit within my body, and the visions of my head troubled me."

This shows that Daniel's reaction was the same after receiving the initial vision and after receiving the more detailed interpretation from the angel. I believe this proves that his troubled state did not improve because of a continued lack of understanding.

Daniel had received a full interpretation of a dream before when he interpreted King Nebuchadnezzar's dream, but now he was struggling to interpret his own vision. This does not speak of Daniel's incompetence, but I believe that God simply did not reveal the whole interpretation to Daniel. I believe that God did not reveal the full interpretation to Daniel because the vision was not for Daniel nor the people of his day but for the people of the last days. The Lord simply used Daniel to receive and write down the vision so that the saints of the last days could read it and understand it. This does not in any form devalue Daniel. He was a godly and powerful prophet. This simply shows us that no matter how gifted or anointed we might be, we can only attain what God reveals to us. Nobody can press into God's mysteries without God giving them the key to His precious treasures. Daniel himself understood this because he spoke this truth to King Nebuchadnezzar:

> Daniel answered in the presence of the king, and said, "The secret which the king has demanded, the wise men, the astrologers, the magicians, and the soothsayers cannot declare to the king. But there is a God in heaven who reveals secrets, and He has made known to King Nebuchadnezzar what will be in the latter days."
>
> Daniel 2:27–28 (NKJV)

So could it be that Daniel simply was used to write down this vision with his limited interpretation so that the last generations could interpret it fully? In chapter twelve of the book of Daniel, we have a similar incident as in chapter seven. Daniel receives another vision about the end times in chapter twelve, and interestingly, this vision has some strong similarities to his vision in chapter seven. After receiving this vision, Daniel says:

"Although I heard, I did not understand. Then I said, 'My lord, what shall be the end of these things?' And he said, 'Go your way, Daniel, for the words are closed up and sealed till the time of the end'" (Daniel 12:8–9, NKJV).

ARE DANIEL'S VISIONS FOR US?

If Daniel did not receive the full interpretations of his visions, the question arises: who will? Could it be that we are this later generation to whom God will reveal more revelation about this vision or even the full meaning of Daniel's vision?

It is no secret that many Christians believe that we are living in the last days. If I look at all that has transpired in the world in just the last thirty years, it certainly looks like we are living in the last days. I am not basing this on my feelings, nor on personal revelation, but rather on what the Bible says about the last days. Some people do not want to be bothered with "last-day warnings" and do not care about what days we are living in. However, I believe that it is important to know the times we live in. It is imperative that we see what is right before our eyes. It is important because if we are indeed in the last days, this would mean that according to *Amos 3:7* and according to *Daniel 12:8–9*, Daniel's end-time vision is no longer sealed but is being revealed to God's prophets and God's people as I am writing this. It would mean that those biblical prophecies apply to us and that in each of those prophecies, there is a measure of understanding for God's people.

Every biblical prophecy embodies wisdom, faith, and direction for God's people. This is not only true for the people who live during the days when the prophecy takes place but also for the people who come before and after. Of course, every biblical prophecy is the most impactful to the people who live in the days that the prophecy speaks about, but think about the people before and after. The people who hear prophecy *before* it happens are blessed by the guidance it releases. The people who read or hear the prophecy *after* it is fulfilled are empowered in their faith and blessed by God's faithfulness. Look at what all the prophecies about Jesus the Messiah did for the people before Jesus came. They gave them hope.

Look at what the prophecies about Jesus the Messiah did for all the people who were there when Jesus walked this earth. They made them believe. Look at what all the prophecies about Jesus being the Messiah are doing for us today. They release faith in us and give us assurance. The visions about Jesus as the Messiah are still leading Jews and unbelievers to Him today. That, my friends, is the power of prophecy. It has affected people in the past, it affects us today, and it will affect us in the future.

For us to know that Daniel's end-time prophecies and visions are for us, we must first attempt to determine if we indeed live in the end times. So, let us look at what men like Daniel, Paul, and even Jesus had to say about the end times.

DO WE LIVE IN THE END TIMES?

"But you, Daniel, shut up the words, and seal the book until the time of the end; many shall run to and fro, and knowledge shall increase" (Daniel 12:4, NKJV).

Daniel was told to shut up the words and to seal them until the time of the end, which will be marked by a great increase in knowledge and business. When we look at God's words in this verse, we realize that His words describe the world that we live in perfectly. The running to and fro, which means great business, is very prevalent these days. No generation before us has ever been as busy. The repercussion of this running around is that people are extremely stressed. Studies show that 55 percent of all Americans suffer from stress due to busy lifestyles.

Just like the Industrial Revolution occurred during the shift between the first and second beasts, so do the technological advancements of the last two decades speak of the shift between the third and the fourth beast. Could it be that the monumental technological advancements of the last thirty years were triggered by a spiritual shift? The invention of the internet has completely changed this world and the way in which we live. Day and night, we are close to our cell phones that connect us to this extremely busy world.

Through the invention of the internet, smartphones, social media, and platforms like YouTube, not only has our busyness increased over the last thirty years or so, but also our knowledge. Like never before in history, knowledge is now at everyone's fingertips. Day or night and halfway across the globe, we have access to knowledge. Day and night, we are bombarded with knowledge and information.

God said to Daniel that the prophetic words of his visions will be shut up until the last days in which there will be a great running around, business, and in which knowledge shall increase. Can you see what is happening before our eyes? Can you see what times we are living exactly in those days that God called "the time of the end"?

PAUL'S END-TIME VISION

Paul also wrote about the end times and gave us a description of how people would behave in the last days:

> But know this, that in the last days perilous times will come: For men will be lovers of themselves, lovers of money, boasters, proud, blasphemers, disobedient to parents, unthankful, unholy, unloving, unforgiving, slanderers, without self-control, brutal, despisers of good, traitors, headstrong, haughty, lovers of pleasure rather than lovers of God, having a form of godliness but denying its power. And from such people turn away!
>
> 2 Timothy 3:1–5 (NKJV)

Let us talk about some of the points that Paul makes here. I am going to be honest: when I read these verses in 2 Timothy, I cannot help but think about the society we live in now. Many people, including many Christians, are lovers of themselves, proud, unthankful, unholy, and unloving. Many churches, some of the biggest ones actually, teach you to love yourself, to follow your own dreams, and to pursue only what makes you happy. That is simply not the Gospel of Jesus Christ. The Western church has very much become an institution that pursues self rather than pursuing God. It has become a group of people that have a *form* of godliness but that deny its power, just as Paul says would take place in the last days. What does this mean? *How* can a person have a form of godliness and deny God's power? *Why* would Christians deny God's power?

There are several reasons why believers deny God's power. One of them is a lack of surrender and denying God's true rule in their lives. Without surrender to God, there is no power of God because an unsurrendered person cannot be trusted by God. If God would give an unsurrendered person His power, they would build their own kingdom with it and not God's kingdom. God lets people build their own kingdom with their own power and reserves His power for those who want to build His kingdom. A person who does not surrender is filled with self. If we are filled with self, what room is left for Jesus in our hearts? What room is left in our temples for the Holy Spirit, the One who gives us power? When we look at the church today, we realize that we see very little of the power of God. Many churches do not witness miracles, many churches do not witness salvations, and many churches look very different than the early Jerusalem church.

Besides a lack of surrender, the church's pursuit of pleasure is to blame. The pursuit of pleasure is more evident in today's church than ever before. Church programs are focused on pleasure, church outreaches are focused on pleasure, and even the messages from pulpits often entail this pursuit of pleasure. Many Western churches pursue pleasure as much as the church of old pursued revival.

These churches are comfortable and cozy, and their leaders never challenge their sheep. There is no conviction in the house of God but an indulgence in worldly things. The focus is on the next fun event, the next pleasure trip, and the next church entertainment.

A soft message is preached to ensure that people will come back the following Sunday. The size of the congregation seems to matter more than the content of the service. People are not being convicted to live a pure life, but they are being assured that everything is fine. Preachers do not want to cause any offense or heaviness. Sin is often ignored and only addressed through motivational messages instead of the preaching of God's Word in power and in truth. Power and truth to be set free, transformed, and renewed. The services are cut as short as possible so that the members can indulge in pleasure for the rest of their Sunday. The worship sets are timed and are more an act of performance rather than an act of worship. Is that not how Paul describes the people of the last days?

"Lovers of pleasure rather than lovers of God, having a form of godliness but denying its power" (2 Timothy 3:4–5, NKJV).

Paul also talks about disobedient children. If we look at the young children of today, I believe that we are looking at the most disobedient generation that this world has ever seen. Many parents are ruled by their children. Parents behave like they are their child's friend, but that is not a parent's job. A parent must be a mother or a father to that child and not its friend. The disobedience in today's youth is a sign of the times that we live in and the pressure of darkness that is coming against every family. Many Christian parents have forgotten what it means to be a parent. All this goes back to the church, which has forgotten to teach godly principles and godly order. It goes back to an end-time church that has forgotten to hold up the truth of God's design for family.

> For the time will come when they will not endure

sound doctrine, but according to their own desires, because they have itching ears, they will heap up for themselves teachers; And they shall turn away their ears from the truth, and shall be turned unto fables.

> 2 Timothy 4:3–4 (NKJV)

The world that we live in is full of people who love money rather than God. In reality, the church is filled with people who love money rather than God. Let us be real and talk about the damage that the prosperity Gospel has brought to the body of Christ. This false Gospel has not just affected the American and European churches, but even the poorest nations in Africa have been infested with it. God indeed is a God who blesses His children, but the prosperity Gospel has gone way too far. Some of the most anointed preachers I have ever met have been bought by this false Gospel, and now they pick people's pockets in the name of Jesus. Years ago, they preached about the spiritual cost of the anointing, and now they preach about the financial cost of their ministry and beg people to give. They use schemes and unbiblical concepts to manipulate people into giving. Are you surprised that this is happening? Paul prophesied about all of this two thousand years ago.

Without going through every word that Paul mentions here, it is clear that his description of the people in the last days is a perfect fit with the world today. Can you see what is right before our eyes? Can you see what times we are living in?

Not every believer fits Paul's description of the unfaithful church. There is a remnant of Christians who truly love and live for Jesus. There are still godly churches all over the Western world that have a heart for revival and for the salvation of the lost. There are still believers who live surrendered lives and who have rejected the pursuit of comfort, pleasure, and their own dreams and instead are tirelessly building God's kingdom. I pray that you are such a believer. I pray that the Holy Spirit would draw you to fully jump into the river of life with no reservations and no holding back. It is worth it!

WHAT JESUS SAID ABOUT THE END TIMES

In the Gospel of Matthew, we find a whole chapter in which Jesus talks to His disciples about the last days.

> Now as He sat on the Mount of Olives, the disciples came to Him privately, saying, "Tell us, when will these things be? And what will be the sign of Your coming, and of the end of the age?"
>
> And Jesus answered and said to them: "Take heed that no one deceives you. For many will come in My name, saying, 'I am the Christ,' and will deceive many. And you will hear of wars and rumors of wars. See that you are not troubled; for all these things must come to pass, but the end is not yet. For nation will rise against nation, and kingdom against kingdom. And there will be famines, pestilences, and earthquakes in various places. All these are the beginning of sorrows."
>
> Matthew 24:3–8 (NKJV)

Look at this world, at all the wars and rumors of wars. Look at all the earthquakes shaking the earth. Look at the pandemics we are experiencing: obesity, diabetes, cancer, high blood pressure, heart disease. Diseases are skyrocketing despite all of the advances in technology and knowledge. Look at all the people who are starving in Africa and Asia. Jesus says that all these signs are the beginning of the end times. He then continues by telling the disciples what will follow next:

> Then they will deliver you up to tribulation and kill you, and you will be hated by all nations for My name's sake. And then many will be offended, will betray one another, and will hate one another. Then many false prophets will rise up and deceive many. And because lawlessness will abound, the love of many will grow cold. But he who endures to the end shall be saved. And this gospel of the kingdom will be preached in all the world as a witness to all the nations, and then the end will come.
>
> Matthew 24:9–14 (NKJV)

When we take in these words and reflect for a moment, we realize that lawlessness is all around us. It is not lawlessness according to the standards of this world, as it seems that this world has no law anymore, but it is lawlessness, first and foremost, according to the standards of God.

Homosexuality, abortion, and transgenderism are the flagships of this lawlessness, but it is abounding in many other areas. This lawlessness is being pushed upon society by the dark forces that are in politics, giant corporations, and the media. We are living in a world that wants to tell us that it is okay to manipulate and permanently change the natural body of children and youth. The same people say a person can now identify as the other sex or even an animal. Who is behind all this? The devil himself. Man was made in God's image, and Satan is mocking God by making humanity, God's beloved creation, mutilate itself. All this and many more things that are happening today speak of a lawlessness that this earth has never seen. Along with this growing lawlessness, we see a steady current in society that is rising up against Christianity and Christian values.

Above all this lawlessness, however, stands another marker of the end times that Jesus mentioned in these verses in Matthew. Jesus prophesied that the love of many would grow cold. Is that not what we are currently witnessing all around us? The love for spouses, the love for kids, the love for God, the love for our nation, and even the love for the most innocent, the unborn. Are we not witnessing that in all these things, the love of many is growing cold?

We have looked at multiple descriptions of the end times from Daniel, Paul, and Jesus Himself. All this leads us to the big question: "Are we living in the end times?" Looking at all these scriptures and other scriptures about the end times, I believe that we are indeed living in the last days. All that being said, I believe that our Heavenly Father will not let us walk blindly into these last days. He has given prophecy so that we know what is happening. He has given us the vision of Daniel chapter seven so that we are aware of what days we live in and so that we may prepare for what is ahead of us and endure.

CHAPTER 11:
IT WAS DIFFERENT FROM THE OTHER BEASTS

COLLECTING DETAILS

Now that we have answered these essential questions, we must start interpreting the fourth beast by briefly collecting the details about it. There are several parts to this final beast that have to be explained. Before reading this chapter, I encourage you to read Daniel chapter seven one more time to refresh all that is recorded in Daniel's vision.

There are essentially four passages in Daniel chapter seven that speak about this fourth beast.

The fourth beast is first mentioned in the initial vision in Daniel 7:7–8 (NKJV):

> After this I saw in the night visions, and behold, a fourth beast, dreadful and terrible, exceedingly strong. It had huge iron teeth; it was devouring, breaking in pieces, and trampling the residue with its feet. It was different from all the beasts that were before it, and it had ten horns. I was considering the horns, and there was another horn, a little one, com-

ing up among them, before whom three of the first horns were plucked out by the roots. And there, in this horn, were eyes like the eyes of a man, and a mouth speaking pompous words.

After that, there is one short section that gives us details about the end of the fourth beast.

> I watched then because of the sound of the pompous words which the horn was speaking; I watched till the beast was slain, and its body destroyed and given to the burning flame. As for the rest of the beasts, they had their dominion taken away, yet their lives were prolonged for a season and a time.
>
> Daniel 7:11–12 (NKJV)

The third time the fourth beast is talked about is when Daniel repeats what he had seen in Daniel 7:19–22 (NKJV):

> Then I wished to know the truth about the fourth beast, which was different from all the others, exceedingly dreadful, with its teeth of iron and its nails of bronze, which devoured, broke in pieces, and trampled the residue with its feet; and the ten horns that were on its head, and the other horn which came up, before which three fell, namely, that horn which had eyes and a mouth which spoke pompous words, whose appearance was greater than his fellows.
> I was watching; and the same horn was making war against the saints, and prevailing against them, until the Ancient of Days came, and a judgment was

made in favor of the saints of the Most High, and the time came for the saints to possess the kingdom.

The fourth and final time that the fourth beast is mentioned is when Daniel receives an interpretation from this heavenly being in Daniel 7:23–27 (NKJV):

> Thus he said: "The fourth beast shall be a fourth kingdom on earth, which shall be different from all other kingdoms, and shall devour the whole earth, trample it and break it in pieces. The ten horns are ten kings who shall arise from this kingdom. And another shall rise after them; He shall be different from the first ones, and shall subdue three kings. He shall speak pompous words against the Most High, shall persecute the saints of the Most High, and shall intend to change times and law. Then the saints shall be given into his hand for a time and times and half a time.
>
> "But the court shall be seated, and they shall take away his dominion, to consume and destroy it forever. Then the kingdom and dominion, and the greatness of the kingdoms under the whole heaven, shall be given to the people, the saints of the Most High. His kingdom is an everlasting kingdom, and all dominions shall serve and obey Him."

IT WAS DIFFERENT FROM ALL THE OTHER BEASTS

After this I saw in the night visions, and behold, a fourth beast, dreadful and terrible, exceedingly strong. It had huge iron teeth; it was devouring, breaking in pieces, and trampling the residue with its feet. It was different from all the beasts that were before it, and it had ten horns.

> Daniel 7:7 (NKJV)

All four beasts were powerful and given dominion over humanity, and each of them changed the world dramatically. Just as the first, second, and third beast ruled for a season, so will the fourth beast rule for a season.

So, how is the fourth beast different from the other three? Let me start with the more obvious differences. The fourth beast appears to be much more powerful than the other three. Daniel describes this fourth beast as dreadful and terrible, which he did not say about the first three. Even though the second beast was commanded to devour much flesh and caused much destruction on earth, the fourth beast will supersede the second beast in causing destruction. Everything about this fourth beast is violent, dark, and extreme. It is dreadful and terrible; it is exceedingly strong, and it has huge iron teeth. All of this makes sense as it is the only beast among the four that turns against God Himself in front of the whole world.

"He shall speak pompous words against the Most High" (Daniel 7:25, NKJV).

None of the other beasts turned publicly against God, nor did they challenge God like this beast will.

THE LAST FIGHT BETWEEN GOOD AND EVIL

At this point in this book, I must reveal one important fact. Under each and every beast, there was a constant battle that was raging: a battle between good and evil.

In the era of the first beast, there were good kings and rulers, and there were evil kings and rulers. The good kings furthered the kingdom of God, while the evil kings furthered the kingdom of darkness. For example, King David furthered God's kingdom while King Herod came against God's kingdom. Emperor Nero built the devil's kingdom while Emperor Constantine brought some light to the Roman Empire.

In the era of the second beast, men like Hitler and Stalin built the kingdom of darkness, while nations like America and Great Britain opposed those kingdoms and were used by God to stop that evil from spreading further. If it had not been for America joining the Second World War, the outcome of Germany and Russia's battle could have been very different, which could have changed the outcome of the entire war. If America had not joined the war, many more Jews would have been murdered, and many more innocent people would have died.

Under the dominion of the third beast, there was also a war between good and evil. Think about the war between capitalism and Communism that captured the entire world. Many people mistake the clash between capitalism and Communism merely as a clash of economic ideas, but the Cold War was not just a war about economic ideologies but; it was a spiritual war between good and evil. One side proclaimed freedom and their trust in God, while the other side brought bondage and wanted to get rid of God. Christianity flourished under capitalism, while Christianity was eradicated under Communism.

When it comes to the fourth beast, this war between good and evil will dramatically shift. The era of the fourth beast will not just be another war between good and evil, but it will be the *final* war between good and evil before Jesus returns. As a matter of fact, it will be Jesus' return that will end this war, and the Antichrist will be defeated.

In this war, before Jesus' return, darkness will overrun the whole earth for the first time in history, as the entire world will be under an evil rule. Before the era of the fourth beast, evil had never had full control of the entire world, only certain territories. Nero built a dark kingdom in one part of the world. Hitler, during the era of the second beast, only brought darkness to parts of this world, but he never had control over the entire world. Russia, under the third beast, brought the dark ideology of Communism to many parts of this world but never had full control over the entire world. This will be very different in the era of the fourth beast.

The vision of Daniel tells us that, for a season, there will be no more opposition to evil on this earth. No nation will oppose this beast, allowing it to rule over the entire earth. From within the fourth beast and its kingdom, ten horns will arise, and after the ten horns, a small horn will arise. This small horn will cause Christians worldwide to suffer heavy persecution. We Christians will continually run, flee, and hide from the persecution of the little horn. All this reveals the very purpose of the fourth beast: to have control over the entire world so that the small horn can unite this fallen world and turn it against the Christians.

> The fourth beast shall be a fourth kingdom on earth, which shall be different from all other kingdoms, and shall devour the whole earth, trample it and break it in pieces. The ten horns are ten kings who shall arise from this kingdom. And another shall rise after them; He shall be different from the first ones, and shall subdue three kings. He shall speak pompous words against the Most High, shall persecute the saints of the Most High, and shall intend to change times and law. Then the saints shall be given into his hand for a time and times and half a time.
>
> Daniel 7:23–25 (NKJV)

The darkness will increase greatly like we have never seen before. It is a troubling thought that this beast will bring more evil to this world than all the world wars, the Holocaust, and Communism together. While this is the reality of what is to come, we must never forget that God will only allow this for a short season. Never forget that God has the ultimate dominion over this world. The only reason why this beast will have such power is because God will permit it. Do not forget, no matter what season, no matter what era, no matter what beast, God is almighty, and God is faithful to His people. God always cares for those who love Him, and He will care for all the precious saints who will have to endure this most dark season.

> Who shall separate us from the love of Christ? Shall tribulation, or distress, or persecution, or famine, or nakedness, or peril, or sword? As it is written:
> "For Your sake we are killed all day long;
> We are accounted as sheep for the slaughter."
> Yet in all these things we are more than conquerors through Him who loved us. For I am persuaded that neither death nor life, nor angels nor principalities nor powers, nor things present nor things to come, nor height nor depth, nor any other created thing, shall be able to separate us from the love of God which is in Christ Jesus our Lord.
>
> Romans 8:35–39 (NKJV)

The beast and the small horn will only be able to destroy the physical lives of the Christians but not their spiritual lives. This is where the Christian faith goes through a fiery trial. This is where the rubber hits the road. There will be strong persecution in those days, but we should never be afraid of persecution. I say this because no one can steal our salvation, and no one can take away the love that our Father has for us.

> "O Death, where is your sting?
> O Hades, where is your victory?"
>
> The sting of death is sin, and the strength of sin is the law. But thanks be to God, who gives us the victory through our Lord Jesus Christ.
>
> Therefore, my beloved brethren, be steadfast, immovable, always abounding in the work of the Lord, knowing that your labor is not in vain in the Lord.
>
> 1 Corinthians 15:55–58 (NKJV)

There will be pain in those days of persecution, but there will also be extreme glory, favor, and love. That is why it is so important for us to be rooted in the Father's love today, as no one knows when those days will come. The Bible tells us, in 1 John 4:18 (NKJV), "There is no fear in love; but perfect love casts out fear, because fear involves torment. But he who fears has not been made perfect in love."

Imagine being one of the apostles who died for Jesus. None of them were afraid when they faced their brutal death. We wonder how this is possible. The answer is that they were filled with perfect love, and there was no room for tormenting fear. This perfect love will be the key for those who will face the persecution of the small horn in the last days.

God will only allow the small horn to rule for a season. Once the rule of the fourth beast hits three and a half years, God will take the beast's power away, take the small horn captive, judge it, and then destroy it. We read all this in Daniel 7:25–26 (NKJV):

He shall speak pompous words against the Most High, shall persecute the saints of the Most High, and shall intend to change times and law. Then the saints shall be given into his hand for a time and times and half a time [three and a half years]. But the court shall be seated, and they shall take away his dominion, to consume and destroy it forever.

A LONG-FOUGHT WAR

We must realize that this war between good and evil, between God and the devil, has been waging for a long time. Satan deceived Eve and all humanity with her in the garden of Eden when she ate from the tree of the knowledge of good and evil. It was the knowledge of good and evil that ushered in the war of good and evil through the power of sin: the sin of disobedience. Since that day in the garden of Eden, many men have chosen to follow the ways of the devil, while others have chosen to follow the ways of God and fight on His side.

Do you remember that there were two trees in the garden of Eden? There was the "tree of the knowledge of good and evil," and then there was the *"tree of life."* It is important to point out that Satan did not deceive Eve to eat the fruit of the *"tree of life"* but only the fruit of the "tree of the knowledge of good and evil." Satan did not deceive Eve to eat from the "tree of life" because Satan did not want humanity to live forever, nor did he want for humanity to live in paradise close to God. The devil wanted humanity to die by being subjected to sin and eternal judgment. He knew that God made men in His own image. It was his hatred and rebellion toward God that motivated him to go after God's most precious creation, us. After sin crept in and men fell, God removed Adam and Eve from the garden so that they would not live forever. Now that sin was part of their nature, He *could not* allow them to live forever.

> Then the Lord God said, "Behold, the man has become like one of Us, to know good and evil. And now, lest he put out his hand and take also of the tree of life, and eat, and live forever"—therefore the Lord God sent him out of the garden of Eden to till the ground from which he was taken.
>
> Genesis 3:22–23 (NKJV)

I believe that, all along, God wanted to protect us from sin. I do not think being a part of this war was His perfect will for us, but when humanity fell into sin, everything changed. God could not allow sinful humanity to live forever. That is why He shut Adam and Eve away from the "tree of life," and He removed them from Eden. Physical death was now a part of men's destiny because sin had become part of humanity first. Eternal judgment became part of humanity's destiny because sin had crept in.

Thank God it did not end there; in God's awesome love and mercy, He came up with a solution for men's grim destiny. Instead of leaving us helpless in our sins and helpless in our death, He gave us a new way to eternal life through the second Adam—His beloved Son Jesus. When humanity fell, we were shut away from the tree of life in the garden of Eden, but because Jesus decided to hang on a tree for our sins, He became our new tree of life. Hallelujah! Through faith in Him and faith in His sacrifice on the cross, we are washed from all sin and can live in eternity with God. All we must do is be born again from our sinful nature, confess Him as our Lord and Savior, and repent from our fallen ways.

TWO TIME PERIODS

The fourth beast is significantly more complex than the three previous beasts. Out of each of the four parts that talk about the fourth beast we can collect valuable details that will help us to break down its complexity and ultimately understand its meaning. The first thing that stands out about the fourth beast is that, unlike the other beasts, this beast manifests itself in two separate time periods:

1. The *"era of the ten horns"* (*also called the ten kings*)
2. The *"era of the little horn"*

"The ten horns are ten kings who shall arise from this kingdom. And another shall rise after them; He shall be different from the first ones, and shall subdue three kings" (Daniel 7:24, NKJV).

It is important that we look at both periods separately in order to understand this beast.

THE FOURTH DIFFERENCE

Now, let's look at the fourth critical difference between the fourth beast and the other beasts. The spirit of Antichrist operated under the first three beasts and raised up antichrists like Nero throughout the centuries. When it comes to the fourth beast, however, this spirit will not just raise up another antichrist, but it will raise up the final Antichrist: *the* Antichrist. The fourth beast must raise up the final Antichrist as this beast will rule in the last hour before Jesus returns. After Jesus' return, there will be no more Antichrist.

"Little children, it is the last hour; and as you have heard that the Antichrist is coming, even now many antichrists have come, by which we know that it is the last hour" (1 John 2:18, NKJV).

Let us now recap the three critical differences of the fourth beast:

1. It will usher in the final war between good and evil.

2. It will have dominion over the entire world, including the saints.

3. It will consist of two separate stages and time periods.

4. The final Antichrist will rise to power during this time.

— CHAPTER 12: —
PREPARING THE WAY

THE PURPOSE OF THE TEN HORNS

Instead of guessing and speculating who these ten horns or ten kings are, I believe it is far more important to identify their purpose according to Daniel's vision. Based on their purpose, it is then a lot easier to understand who those ten horns are. This book is not a "thus says the Lord" prophecy book, and in my opinion, there are too many people out there who put God's name on everything. While I believe that God still speaks clearly to His people, I also believe that we must be extremely careful when we put God's name on anything.

I believe the purpose of the ten horns is very straightforward. The purpose of the ten horns is to prepare the way for the final Antichrist. Just like John the Baptist prepared the way for our Savior, Jesus Christ, these horns prepare the way for the final Antichrist. I believe that these ten horns are ten movements that shape humanity for the coming of the little horn—the final Antichrist. I do not believe that the ten horns are actually ten kings or ten actual persons, but rather that the kings in Daniel's vision represent the power that these ten movements will have. I say this because in Daniel 7:20 (NKJV), we read, "And the ten horns that were on its head, and the other horn which came up, before which three fell, namely, that horn which had eyes and a mouth which spoke pompous words, whose appearance was greater than his fellows."

If the ten horns were kings in the flesh, actual persons, then why would the scripture differentiate the little horn by saying that it had eyes and a mouth and spoke pompous words? If all the horns were persons why is the little horn differentiated by having eyes and a mouth? To me, this makes it clear that the little horn is the only one out of the eleven horns that is a person. Instead of being persons, these ten horns are movements that have a great effect on humanity.

I believe that these ten movements are, in fact, so powerful that they will change the way humanity thinks and how humanity will perceive the truth. These movements will break down the line between what is right and wrong. Think about it: in order for the world to receive the Antichrist, people will have to have been previously acclimated to spiritual darkness, lies, and deception. For him to be accepted by the world, he will have to flow with the existing spiritual current upon his arrival. Just as Hitler perfectly fit into the spiritual current of Germany after World War I, the final Antichrist will fit perfectly into this world when he rises to power.

In second Thessalonians chapter two, we read about how the world will be prepared for the final Antichrist. In the last days, the truth will be undermined, and many will be deceived before the coming of *the lawless one*, the final Antichrist.

> And then the lawless one will be revealed, whom the Lord will consume with the breath of His mouth and destroy with the brightness of His coming. The coming of the lawless one is according to the working of Satan, with all power, signs, and lying wonders, and with all unrighteous deception among those who perish, because they did not receive the love of the truth, that they might be saved. And for this reason

God will send them strong delusion, that they should believe the lie, that they all may be condemned who did not believe the truth but had pleasure in unrighteousness.

2 Thessalonians 2:8–12 (NKJV)

The lawless one is the Antichrist. His end, described here in Thessalonians, fits perfectly with the ending of the little horn described in Daniel chapter seven.

"The coming of the lawless one is according to the working of Satan, with all power, signs, and lying wonders, and with all unrighteous deception" (2 Thessalonians 2:9–10, NKJV).

Here, we learn that the very coming of the Antichrist will happen according to the work of Satan. This speaks of a preparation that happens before the final Antichrist comes. Signs, lying wonders, and deception will be released upon the world. This preparation work will be conducted by the spirit of Antichrist, who will use ten dark movements to prepare humanity for absolute darkness.

THE TEN HORNS—THE TEN MOVEMENTS

What are the ten horns? What are these ten steps that the spirit of Antichrist will have to take to prepare for the coming of the final Antichrist? What follows are the movements that have already occurred, that are happening, and that will unfold until the Antichrist appears. I believe that each movement's purpose is to prepare for the coming of the final Antichrist. In order to prepare the way, each movement must, on the one hand, undermine the one true King, Jesus Christ, and on the other hand, prepare the Antichrist's coming by blinding the world.

The First Horn—Counterfeit Religion

The first big movement that started the preparation for the Antichrist's coming was and is the movement of counterfeit religion. Religions like Hinduism, Buddhism, Islam, Mormonism, the Jehovah's Witnesses, and many other smaller and pagan religions have spread all over the world since this movement began. All these religions are to distract people from recognizing that Jesus is the only Savior of mankind. No one but God Himself would be able to count the number of people in the history of mankind who have rejected Jesus Christ as their Savior because of counterfeit religion. These people have either been preoccupied with counterfeit religion so that when the true Gospel was shared with them, they did not receive it, or they were snatched away by a false religion after having received the Gospel. In either scenario, counterfeit religion has been, without a doubt, the devil's longest and most successful movement to turn people away from Jesus. The very spirit of Antichrist is in every counterfeit religion, and this spirit will continue to use false religion in the last days.

The Second Horn—Humanism

Humanism is another movement that took hold of the entire world, predominately in Western Christian nations. Humanism places an emphasis on the human realm. The foundational thought is that man is worshiped but not God the Creator. The creature is worshiped but not God. It denies divinity and the realm of the supernatural. At its core is the desire to pursue only human virtues but not God's virtues.

Just like the movement of counterfeit religion, humanism is very much alive today. If anything, I would say that it is more alive today than ever before. Most unbelievers and even believers have been manipulated by this movement. The word "humanism" made it into our history books way back in the mid-thirteenth century, even though its sinful core goes all the way back to the fall of men itself. In the mid-thirteenth century, in the Italian city of Florence, several men birthed this movement. Since then, humanism has spread all over the world in many different forms.

The men who were behind this movement thought that they were extremely wise, but in reality, they were just played by the spirit of Antichrist. The humanists' mission was to reform the existing Christian culture of medieval times by going back to ancient Greek and Roman thought. They found great excitement and purpose in these pagan religions. Amazingly, Paul the Apostle wrote about all of this in his epistle to the Roman church. Paul identified that spirit already back then and was led by the Holy Spirit to address this issue with the Roman church. Think about it: Paul wrote this to the church of the Roman Empire. Centuries later, in the city of Florence, which was part of the Roman Empire in Paul's time, the spirit of Antichrist birthed a worldwide movement with the same wrong doctrine that Paul already had addressed in Romans 1:22–27 (NKJV):

> Professing to be wise, they became fools, and changed the glory of the incorruptible God into an image made like corruptible man—and birds and four-footed animals and creeping things.
>
> Therefore God also gave them up to uncleanness, in the lusts of their hearts, to dishonor their bodies among themselves, who exchanged the truth of God for the lie, and worshiped and served the creature rather than the Creator, who is blessed forever. Amen.
>
> For this reason God gave them up to vile passions. For even their women exchanged the natural use for what is against nature. Likewise also the men, leaving the natural use of the woman, burned in their lust

for one another, men with men committing what is shameful, and receiving in themselves the penalty of their error which was due.

It is almost shocking to read these verses. With every line, Paul gives a perfect description of humanism. The men under this Antichrist spirit of humanism were puffed up in their arrogant minds, and instead of worshiping the only incorruptible God, they worshiped themselves, the corruptible man. In the last verses, Paul says that because of their "humanist" corruption, God gave them up to uncleanness. Out of that very uncleanness, homosexuality came upon the people. This sin was already practiced before Paul's address, for example, in Sodom and Gomorrah. History, however, confirms Paul's words about homosexuality being a fruit of humanism in a far more shocking way.

Homosexuality in the fifteenth century became rampant in the city of Florence, Italy. The very city that is called the birthplace of organized humanism, the very city that so openly embraced humanism, was, in return, overrun with homosexual sin. This homosexual movement became so strong that the government of Florence started to hunt down homosexual men. They formed a group called "Officers of the Night" that would patrol through the streets and the city to catch men practicing homosexuality. Florence became so widely known for its homosexuality that in the German Renaissance movement, homosexuals were actually called "Florencers."

The influence of humanism has not become weaker, nor did it stop with the end of the Renaissance age. Humanism is behind all philosophy that is at its very core anti-Christian. Humanism is also the power behind the theory of evolution. This theory goes against God, and its aim is to put doubt into people's hearts. Doubt about the Creator. If a person believes that there is no Creator, the same person will believe that there is no Savior either.

Today, we see humanism everywhere. Society has fully embraced it. Life is all about us humans, what we can do, and what we want to do. Everyone is free to live out their desires, whether they are right or wrong. Society believes that it is we humans who will "save" the planet and we humans who have the future of mankind in our hands. Sadly, society has forgotten that we humans are weak and hopeless in our own strength. We do not have anything to say about the future of this planet or this world. None of these things are in humanity's hands, but humanity would be in a better place if we would remember that we are nothing but dust in God's almighty hand. It is He who has this world and all of our lives in His most capable hands.

The Third Horn—Counterfeit Ideology

I have already written a lot about counterfeit ideology in this book, so I will keep this portion short. This movement was and is the devil's avenue for all those who have rejected religion altogether. Wrong ideologies like Communism, nationalism, and atheism have deceived millions and millions of people in the history of mankind. This movement is and was so powerful that it has also affected the Christian church.

Germany was a Christian nation counting around forty million Protestants and twenty million Catholics when Hitler and his Nazi party came to power. Yet, the large majority of the German church did not oppose Hitler's evil ideology but actually embraced it almost instantly. The longer Hitler was in power, the more Christians fell for his ideology. Nationalism very quickly became more important than Christianity. The love of self and the love of the German nation became far more important than loving the neighboring countries. Nationalism goes against some of the most foundational Christian values, to love our neighbors like ourselves. The German church, however, did not detect this grave error in nationalism but received it, received Hitler, and some even went so far as to compare Hitler to Jesus.

As I mentioned previously, Communism, another ideology of the third horn, has destroyed many Christian nations in history. While pure Communism is not as evident today, this ideology has adapted and mixed with other dangerous ideologies. There are many variances of this ideology, but all go back to the same author, the spirit of Antichrist. One offshoot is socialism. People say: "What is wrong about socialism?"

Socialism is a mixture of Communism and humanism, and it is very sly. The door that socialism uses is the helping of less fortunate people, but what the enemy is using it for is to make people dependent on the government rather than God. The social policies take care of the poor instead of Christian compassion that points to the Savior. The government becomes the provider instead of Jehovah Jireh. In return for receiving the benefits of the social programs, people give up their freedom.

There is nothing wrong with helping the poor and helping those in need. In fact, the Bible tells us to do just that, but here is what I have seen. Since the rise of socialism in nations like Germany, Denmark, and Sweden, there always has been a strong departure from God and Christian values. Since humanism and atheism are packaged into socialism, the nations and people under it eventually depart more and more from godly values and God Himself. I grew up in Germany, and I have seen the destructive power of socialism, humanism, and atheism over just the last twenty years. Today, in Germany, reports show the lowest number of Christians in all of Germany's history. When you look at the numbers, you will find that the ten most atheist countries in the world are either socialist, Communist, or ex-Communist nations.

This is not a coincidence but a clear sign of who is behind these ideologies. There is a reason why a person cannot find a socialist party anywhere in the world with strong Christian values.

The Fourth Horn—The Departure from Truth

"The coming of the lawless one is according to the working of Satan, with all power, signs, and lying wonders, and with all unrighteous deception among those who perish, because they did not receive the love of the truth, that they might be saved" (2 Thessalonians 2:10, NKJV).

The main reason why people will follow the Antichrist is because, by the time he appears, humanity will have lost its love for the truth. The majority of people, including many Christians, will have departed from the truth. This is the mission of this fourth movement. It will bring darkness, confusion, and false information to mess up the moral compass of right and wrong. This movement is already in full swing, and on many levels of society, truth has been compromised. That the unsaved will reject truth does not come as a huge surprise, but what shocks me to the core today is the stand of the church when it comes to truth.

Is it not interesting that the Bible does *not* say, "Among those who perish, because they did not have love" or "Among those who perish, because they did not have truth."

But the Bible says, "Among those who perish, because they did not receive *the love of the truth*" *(2 Thessalonians 2:10, NKJV).*

This is an amazing key for us as Christians on how to protect ourselves from deception in these last days. We all know that we are commanded to love God, to love one another, and to even love our enemy. Even though it is vital for us to love and even though love is the mark of the true follower of Christ, the Bible reveals here that love alone will not keep us from falling away from God in the last days. Based on these verses in Thessalonians, God does not require us to have *all* truth, but in order to be protected in the last days, we must have a *love for the truth.* God does not call us to have all truth because only He has all truth.

It is impossible for us, inhabitants of this fallen world, to have all truth. What He wants for us is to love truth. It is the love for truth that will keep us safe from falling away because if you have a love for the truth, this love will always pull you like a magnet to God. This love for the truth speaks of an upright heart that desires to find God's truth in every situation. Instead of giving us *all* truth in one heaping, God desires to have a relationship with us in which He can lead us to the truth about everything. It speaks of a constant connection to Him and a constant growing in Him. The ones who love Him, the ones who are committed to Him, and the ones who are in covenant with Him will naturally have a love for His truth. And that truth will be instrumental to staying clear of the deception and the false doctrines of the last days. If we do not have a love for truth, even today, we are in great danger of being deceived. Truth is a shield and an armor that protects us from being deceived.

Every time truth is presented to us, we should embrace it because we should love truth. Jesus said in John 14:6 (NKJV) these most famous words: "I am the way, the truth, and the life. No one comes to the Father except through Me."

The sequence in which Jesus said this is no coincidence. In between the way and the life is the word "truth." Without truth, the way and the life will never connect. We cannot bypass the truth because Jesus is all three. He is the way, He is the truth, and He is the life. On our way to eternal life with our heavenly Father must be truth. It is what keeps us on the narrow path that leads to life. Without truth, there would be no salvation because it is realizing the truth about ourselves and about Jesus that saves us. The truth is that we all were hopeless sinners in need of the Savior. If Jesus is the truth and if He truly lives inside of us, should we not love the truth and not turn away from it during our life here on earth?

There has been a frightening shift in the body of Christ when it comes to the truth of scripture. It does not matter what church you step into; you will always hear about the love of God. No matter what nation or what denomination you are in, you will always hear about His love. Praise the Lord! God's love is of utmost importance. It is so amazing that it must be talked about, especially to the unsaved, the discouraged, and the depressed. My question, however, is the following: "Can the same be said about His truth?" Do you hear the same emphasis on truth?

There has been a stark decline in pursuing truth in the body of Christ. A decline that I believe we, as a church, have never seen before. We are coming to a place as a body where the line between right and wrong is becoming blurred. What used to be wrong is not necessarily called *right* in many churches, but it is also not called wrong in many churches. The "gray zone" of truth is widening, and if that course is not corrected, what follows next is a widespread abandonment of the truth, which is exactly what the Antichrist needs. Parts of society are still looking toward the church to find truth, but if the church continues to compromise the preaching of the truth many people within and without the church will fall away.

We all know that this complete abandonment of truth has happened in some parts of the body already. We know that it has happened when we hear of homosexual pastors (obvious heresy) and when we witness a complete departure from scripture. While some churches have totally walked away from God's truth and are now openly practicing sin, I would say that the majority of the Western church does not go to that extreme. The problem is not that the majority of the church practices obvious sin, but the problem is that the majority of the church simply avoids speaking God's truth without compromise. Sadly, many churches simply avoid making that stand because they will lose members.

Truth has been the one uncomfortable thing that stands in conflict with the seeker-friendly movement of the Western church. The church would rather speak about love than confront people with truth, but let me ask you this: what is love without truth? We are witnessing pastors who avoid speaking against the most obvious sins like abortion, Christians who avoid confronting homosexuality as a sin, families who disregard God's order for family, and so on. Truth, however, is not just lacking in these big-ticket items. No, it goes a lot deeper than that.

Many Christians will say, "As long as we all believe that Jesus is the Son of God and that He died for us, all is good. All the other things don't matter. They just cause disunity." I can't tell how many times I have heard this. It shakes me to the core because it goes against every fiber of who Jesus is. He embodies all truth. Yes, His ministry here on earth was to proclaim the powerful truth that He is the Son of God and that He came to save us, but He also taught many other life-bringing truths to humanity.

"For I rejoiced greatly when brethren came and testified of the truth that is in you, just as you walk in the truth. I have no greater joy than to hear that my children walk in truth" (3 John 1:3–4, NKJV).

In these words from apostle John, it is clear to see that truth is intertwined in every aspect of the Christian life, in everything we do and in everything we believe. Truth is one of the key pillars of Christianity, and it must stand resolute in all aspects of Christian living. If not, the devil will conquer one aspect of the Christian life at a time, and at the end, he will even be able to uproot the very cornerstone—Jesus Christ Himself. The Antichrist will come with lying signs and wonders and even appear as an angel of light, and only those who love the truth and embrace the precious Spirit of truth will be able to discern between false and true.

"And for this reason God will send them strong delusion, that they should believe the lie, that they all may be condemned who did not believe the truth but had pleasure in unrighteousness" (2 Thessalonians 2:11–12, NKJV).

Those in the church who will not cultivate a love for the truth in these trying days that we live in now will only fall further and further away in the days to come. God Himself will send to those who don't have a love for truth strong delusion. Multitudes of

Christians will start to believe lies, false doctrine, and false theories that will lead them into condemnation. They will be perceptive to what the spirit of this world is fabricating through media and false information. The currents of the world will grab those Christians who are not founded in God's truth and take them with them in following strong delusions. There has been a dramatic increase in delusions in the last years that society and the church have blindly accepted. This increase will not stop, nor will it slow down, but keep going until the strongest delusion of them all, the Antichrist, reveals himself.

Dear reader, I encourage you to seek God's truth with your whole heart. Remain in His word daily and cultivate your relationship with the Holy Spirit, the Spirit of truth. Don't give in to the pressures that try to push you to live in the gray zones. Don't be afraid to offend people by preaching God's truth in love. Let your speech be always gracious but seasoned with salt.

"Let your speech always be with grace, seasoned with salt, that you may know how you ought to answer each one" (Colossians 4:6, NKJV).

The Fifth Horn — Turning Hearts Cold

Jesus said, in Matthew 24:12–14 (NKJV), "And because lawlessness will abound, the love of many will grow cold. But he who endures to the end shall be saved. And this gospel of the kingdom will be preached in all the world as a witness to all the nations, and then the end will come."

In these verses, Jesus gives us an amazing description of the environment that love needs. God's love flourishes in a nation among people who honor and follow God's law. Any group of people or nation that rejects God's perfect law will also depart from God's love. Because of lawlessness, because of the fourth movement (the departure of truth), and because of the lack of God's law, the hearts of many will grow cold in this world. I believe that this move of turning people's hearts cold is already happening before our eyes. This is because this world is already walking away from God's law in leaps of rebellion. This world is becoming more and more lawless day by day. This fifth horn is changing law and the presumption of morality so that when the final Antichrist rises to power, he can lead the world into absolute lawlessness. Whatever love in this world will be left at that point will be completely swallowed up when the Antichrist's law is established. The Christians will be the only ones who will be carriers of true love.

"He shall speak pompous words against the Most High, shall persecute the saints of the Most High, and shall intend to change times and law" (Daniel 7:25, NKJV).

Look at the work of this fifth horn; look at what is happening before our eyes. We are witnessing a coldness toward babies and children. We are witnessing a coldness toward the elderly. We are witnessing a coldness between husbands and wives. I do not believe that this world has ever faced such coldness before. It is because love is the driving force of all life. In it, everything good is found. In it, hope is found. In it, peace is found, and most importantly, in love, Jesus is found. The Antichrist cannot rule over a world full of hope and love, but he needs a world that is lost in darkness, cold, and confused. A world that will see him as the savior when he appears. The Antichrist knows that without love, we are sunk. Our relationship with Jesus is based on love, as is our relationship with our spouse. What holds our families, churches, and communities together? Love.

That is why love is under attack and why true love is becoming more and more rare. While this movement of the spirit of Antichrist is making this world colder and colder, we, as Christians, have a unique opportunity to build the kingdom of God like never before. If we are true recipients of God's love in this cold season, we will be able to reach many with God's life-changing love. Humanity has always looked for and craved love, and the contrast between love and hate has never been stronger than today. Do not be discouraged! Ask for His love, receive His love, and show His love to others. His love in this cold world stands out like never before. Go out, love like Jesus, and spread it: many are looking for it.

The Sixth Horn—Restriction of Freedom

Freedom threatens everything that the final Antichrist intends to do. The sixth horn's mission is to undermine and limit freedom worldwide so that the Antichrist can rise to power. Over the last years, freedom worldwide has been under immense attack. Throughout the COVID-19 epidemic, we have seen even our freedom to make medical decisions over our own bodies infringed upon. Vaccines were forced upon certain groups of people, and when they rejected the vaccine, people lost their essential freedoms. During COVID-19, we also lost our freedom to go to church, and our freedom to travel was infringed upon. This has not happened before in the history of our country or in the history of many other nations.

In the last few decades, many nations across the world have lost more and more of their freedoms in a destructive trade-off with socialism. No other nation, however, has been under more pressure to give up its freedom than the United States of America. The sixth horn is pushing, and the pressure is piling up on us from every side. Europe is pushing, Canada is pushing, and even from within our own nation, large groups of people and politicians are pushing for us to give up on our God-given freedoms. People from other nations do not really understand how important our freedom is. Many people in other nations think that they are free because they can live out their (mostly sinful) desires, but they have never tasted true freedom. True freedom goes a lot deeper than that.

True freedom comes from our heavenly Father. He does not give us freedom to live sinful lives, but He gives freedom from the bondage that enslaves us. He gives us freedom from any form of spiritual captivity so that we can follow Jesus Christ and preach the Gospel in power.

Upon that very freedom, America was built, separate from the bondage that was upon the people in Europe and separate from the bondage that European governments wanted to impose on America. The settlers were people who wanted to be free, and that is why they left to build a new world. The motivation to leave home and to build a new world was largely to escape religious persecution and to experience true religious freedom. It was not for freedom to depart from Christianity but freedom to follow Christ.

It is that very freedom that is under attack today. America is being ridiculed and pressured by the nations today because of the stand for independence that it made a few hundred years ago. This was not just another revolution, but I believe it was a sovereign move of God. He has a purpose for America, but in order for this purpose to be fulfilled, America must remain free.

Americans who have never lived in other nations of the world have little to no idea what they actually have in this great nation. I myself have lived and traveled all over Europe and Canada, and I have traveled all over Africa. I have never experienced as much freedom as I have here in the United States. The freedom that we have here does not just come from nowhere; it comes from God. When that freedom leaves, dependence on God leaves because dependence on the government is established. That is what I see happening in many European nations and also nations like Canada and Australia.

If the government becomes ungodly and is unwilling to say, "In God we trust," then the decline of that nation is inevitable. Every nation that is losing its freedoms right now is being moved by the sixth horn. The pressure that is coming against America from within and without is the working of the same horn. It is preparing this world to be ruled by ungodly governments that infringe upon God-given freedoms. Every nation that will remain free is singled out, and the pressure upon such a nation will intensify. Do you think it is a coincidence that the two most pressured nations today are the United States and Israel?

Every nation that does not go with the current of this fallen world will be singled out, pressured, and infiltrated until that nation gives in and goes with the flow. Daniel's vision makes it very clear that the Antichrist will rule over the entire earth, which means that there will not be one independent free nation when he rules.

"The fourth beast shall be a fourth kingdom on earth, which shall be different from all other kingdoms, and shall devour the whole earth, trample it and break it in pieces" (Daniel 7:23, NKJV).

Nations are currently falling in line one by one. Specifically, the nations in the Western world are being targeted by this horn. Most nations in Asia and Africa already lost their freedom a long time ago through the movements of counterfeit ideology and counterfeit religion. The remaining free countries in Africa are being devoured by a greedy Communist China.

I believe that when America loses its freedom, the reign of the Antichrist will be very close. That being said, this nation has a purpose and a job yet to fulfill. I believe this purpose is to hold up the mandate of freedom until every nation, every tribe, and every ear has heard the good news of the Gospel. The United States also has a mandate from God to protect and defend the nation of Israel. Why does the United States have so much authority all over the world? I believe it is because God has given this mandate to the United States. Because of ungodly politicians, movements, and a sleeping American church, this authority has weakened over the years, but this does not mean that it has to stay like that. I believe there is grace for the American Church and people to raise up again to our former strength so that the Gospel will be preached across the globe like never before.

If we want to change the America of today, we must change the church of America first. Revival has never been more needed than today. Just as Nehemiah built a wall around Jerusalem, so must the American church wake up and build a spiritual wall around this nation. The Holy Spirit wants to use men and women, young and old, to bring revival to this barren land. God gave America freedom not to become complacent but to be passionate and active for the sake of His kingdom here on earth. The hate of the enemy and the hate of many ungodly governments are raging against the United States because it still stands for freedom and godly values, and we must not give in any further. Even though there has been a strong decline in Christianity in recent years, I believe America is still one nation under God, and I still see a large majority of Christians who will not back down. This, to me, is a strong indication that God is not done yet with America.

I believe He wants to use this nation for one last worldwide revival, but first, *we* must be revived. When God called me to America, He said, "Go to America and preach the gospel, for My people are confused." That has been my mission here, and that will be my mission until God moves me on. I believe God is raising up other men and women who He will use to bring clarity and spiritual health back to these lands. We need a fresh move of God, and this move starts with you and me.

The Seventh Horn — Destruction of Family

We all know that family is a blessing from our heavenly Father. God knew that it was not good for Adam to be alone, so He created Eve. One of the fruits of this covenant relationship between a husband and a wife is to have offspring together. A family is a powerful and intimate union of people. For this union to be fruitful, however, it must be set up according to God's perfect order. Today, many people cringe when they hear the word "order." To some, it comes across as an almost evil word from the olden days. It seems like a forgotten and overrated principle from previous generations. "The days of order are over" is what many people and even Christians think. They think that because times have changed and culture has changed, having order is no longer necessary. Unfortunately, that is a dangerous misunderstanding. God's order of things will never change, His ways will always be straight, His gate to life will always be narrow, and His principles will stand resolute for all eternity.

"For I am the Lord, I do not change" (Malachi 3:6, NKJV).

"Jesus Christ is the same yesterday, today, and forever" (Hebrews 13:8, NKJV).

If the traditions of men are allowed to alter just one word in the scriptures, then scripture no longer has power. Culture, traditions, and human preferences must never change God's written Word. The Bible actually warns us about this very thing.

"Making the word of God of no effect through your tradition which you have handed down. And many such things you do" (Mark 7:13, NKJV).

God's order is perfect, and His order will always produce life. A fruitful life is a life that is lived according to God's order. When it comes to family, God's design is very clear. He created the man to be the head of the family and the head of the wife. God created the wife to be the man's helper in all he does and to support him in all that God has called him to do. God created the children to be submitted to the father and the mother and to honor them for all of their lives. Together, parents raise their children to become steadfast, godly, and strong Christians. That is God's perfect order. If a family lives according to this order, such a family will flourish, and their actions will honor God.

Why did God set up such a strong order in regard to the family, you may wonder? There are three key attributes that are found in this union of family according to God's order. These three attributes decide between life and death. If the order of the family is messed up, the children, the next generation, will suffer terribly. A godly family model sets kids up for life, but an ungodly family model has the potential to destroy them for life. Let us quickly look at the three attributes that come from a healthy family.

Protection

In God's perfect order for family, absolute protection is found for each family member. The head of the husband is Christ, and therefore, it is Jesus Himself who protects the husband spiritually. If the husband, however, does not function or behave as the head of his family, such a husband forfeits his protection. Only a husband who stands in his rightful place will receive protection from his head, Jesus.

The head of the wife is the husband, a huge responsibility that many men neglect. As a husband, the man is called to cover his wife spiritually and physically. A wife who is not submitted makes a mistake, as she leaves her place of protection. When it comes to children, both parents provide protection. The mother's form of protection is primarily found in her nurturing of the kids, while the father's form of protection is primarily spiritual and physical. The mother has intuition, which also provides an important layer of spiritual protection around her kids.

Security (Identity)

When I say security, I do not mean the security that comes from protection but from identity. In God's perfect order of family, life-giving identity is found. The father is, once again, the one who really sets this into motion, as identity always comes from the father. That is why, throughout all of history, people have referred to themselves as "so-and-so's son or daughter."

Parents work together to provide identity for their children. It is really important that kids have a strong understanding of who they are. When they think about their family, in their hearts and minds, there should be a clear understanding of what the family stands for and who they are as a family. Identity comes from identifying what God has placed into a child's life. The responsibility of the parents is to identify the personality of their child, as well as the giftings and callings upon their child, to relay them to the child and to call them forth. The heavenly Father also entrusts parents with building their child's character according to the calling He has placed on the child. Lastly, parents are called to lead their child toward Jesus Christ, who then will lead the child to His heavenly Father, the source of all security, value, and identity. To be a parent is a huge but also amazing job. There are very few things as rewarding as giving a child identity by raising them according to God's order.

Guidance (Leadership)

The husband and father leads the wife and mother. Together, they then lead the children. It is instrumental for children to learn about leadership and to submit to leadership. Parents who fail in this task will inevitably raise rebellious kids. It is the proud who will resist authority, and under no circumstances do we want to raise prideful and rebellious children. A lack of leadership or ungodly leadership will create rebellion, and rebellion will cause a lack of identity for a child. Rebellion is a counterfeit of identity, as a rebellious person's identity is entirely founded upon standing against everything. This person will literally have no likes or dislikes of their own but always swim against the current, no matter what.

Rebellion is only one of many wrong fruits that ungodliness or lack of leadership will produce. In leadership, guidance is found, and it is guidance that children desperately need. This is true for babies, toddlers, kids, teenagers, young adults, and adults. A wrong leadership model between the father and the mother or the parents and their kids will cause a lot of damage to the kids. Guidance will produce the growth that children need to flourish in this fallen world.

Now that I have talked about the importance of God's order, a godly family, and the function of each member of the family, I want to highlight the purpose of the seventh horn. This horn's purpose is to break up the family model that God has designed. The devil knows the power of unity, the power of God's order, and the power of family. He understands that by breaking up the family structure, he will have access to the next generation. He knows that the children in a family that is in godly order are protected. He knows they have identity, and he knows that they have guidance. What he is looking for is a generation of people who are not protected and who have no identity nor guidance so that he can deceive them to follow the Antichrist. This is the seventh horn's mission, and it has been extremely successful in the Western world.

We are looking at a generation that consists of many weak and spineless men, husbands and fathers who are delinquent and distracted, and women who run the family. This is the perfect storm as this evil model gets passed on from one generation to the next generation. With every generation, more people fall into this trap. Shockingly, many Christians and churches have adopted this ungodly model even though the scriptures are abundantly clear about this.

Have you noticed the strong current that flows against men in this culture that we live in? Many advertisements, many movies, and many songs have given a platform to the mission of the seventh horn. Once the man's role is undermined, the devil has full access to women and children. Weak men are celebrated, and strong men are ridiculed and attacked.

Allow me to give you a picture of Jesus as He truly was here on earth. He was meek and humble, but He was a strong man. Jesus actually was a builder rather than a carpenter, which meant He was working with heavy materials like stone and timber. Jesus was extremely compassionate, yet He was always truthful, direct, and unmovable. He was very loving, but yet He was a strong leader unto all the people who followed Him. He endured discomfort, hunger, and thirst, and He endured much emotional and physical pain. To me, Jesus paints the perfect picture of what a man is called to be and what every man should aspire to be.

Today's culture paints, however, a completely different picture, and unfortunately, many women and many men have adapted to this Antichrist-inspired picture of a man. Weak, compromising, lukewarm, irresponsible, emotional, elusive, unstable, and insecure males are what the seventh horn wants and what culture has accepted. It is time for godly men to raise up in the full image of their Creator, without compromise and without apology. Ladies, encourage your husbands to stand tall in their true purpose as men, inspire your sons to become strong like their fathers, and by doing that, fulfill your calling as a helpmate and a friend to your husbands and a mother to your sons.

The Eighth Horn—World Peace

This fallen world is crying out for peace, but unfortunately, it is looking in all the wrong places. I do believe that one of the Antichrist's missions will be to fulfill the world's desire for peace. For the very reason that he will establish peace, the nations will accept him and follow him. The peace that the Antichrist will bring will not be true peace but counterfeit peace. The only true peace this world can find is in the arms of Jesus. Only under His rule and caring love can we find peace and rest for our souls.

The eighth horn's purpose is to prepare the world for the counterfeit peace of the Antichrist. The horn's mission is to corrupt how people perceive peace. Once it has been successful, it will make them chase its counterfeit peace.

For many years, humanity has been indoctrinated that there must be peace. From a young age, we are being told that the most important thing is to have peace in this world. While true peace in itself is beautiful, godly, and worthwhile to pursue, we must never forget that only through Jesus can the world find true peace.

No treaty, no policy, and no contract can manufacture the peace that Jesus brings. None of these human approaches will ever establish long-lasting peace, but everything that is made in human strength and wisdom will fall. What God establishes lasts forever. The peace that a person can receive through Jesus is complete and will last for all of eternity. God's peace is the fruit of grace. It produces righteousness, is birthed in truth, and only exists in absolute forgiveness.

The peace that this world is seeking is very different and comes from compromise. This eighth horn is teaching people to compromise and tolerate to achieve peace. While Jesus changes people from the inside out so that they can find peace, this horn lies to the people and tells them to compromise to achieve peace rather than pursuing what is right and true in order to have peace. This movement compromises the penalty of sin and the meaning of life so that people can have a sense of peace. When there is no more clear sin and when people stop searching for the truth in life, the world will have a sense of peace.

Everyone who does not compromise or call sin out is an enemy of this movement. This might shock you, but tolerance is not a Christian value. Tolerance means to accept behavior or positions that go against our own opinion. While our personal opinions of things are often skewed or heavily influenced by previous experiences and subject to not being true, that cannot be said about God's Word and principles. It is good to be tolerant of things that God gives us freedom in, but it is not good to be tolerant of things that go against God's law and His order. If a person likes different food, music, or clothing than us, we should be tolerant of that. If a person endorses sin and lives out sinful behavior, we should not be tolerant of that. Our responsibility as Christians is to tell that person the truth in love and offer to guide them out of that sinful behavior.

I believe the time is near when true Christians will be officially called peace disturbers because we will not back down from what we know to be true, right, and noble. I believe we will be called peace disturbers because we will not stop proclaiming the necessity of the work of the cross. The eighth horn's purpose is to turn people against Christians. It is painting the Christians as the enemies just like the spirit of Antichrist used Hitler to paint the Jews as the enemy. That is not all that the eighth horn is doing. This horn's purpose is also to compromise the church's stand of understanding true peace.

In the sixth chapter of Jeremiah, we read how God warns the Jews through His prophet Jeremiah of the coming destruction of Jerusalem through the Babylonian army. There are a lot of similarities between the Jerusalem described in Jeremiah chapter six and the church today.

> They dress the wound of my people as though it were not serious. "Peace, peace," they say, when there is no peace. Are they ashamed of their detestable conduct? No, they have no shame at all; they do not even know how to blush. So they will fall among the fallen; they will be brought down when I punish them.
>
> Jeremiah 6:14–15 (NIV)

Let me tell you something profound: God is not afraid to fight for what is right. God is not afraid of war, nor does He want His children to be afraid. We are not called to make peace with everyone, but we are called to fight a spiritual war. This war is not against flesh and blood but against the powers of darkness.

"For we wrestle not against flesh and blood, but against principalities, against powers, against the rulers of the darkness of this world, against spiritual wickedness in high places" (Ephesians 6:12, NKJV).

Have you ever considered yourself to be a warrior of God's army? If not, it is time for you to realize that God called you to be a warrior. Just because we are not called to fight against flesh and blood does not mean that we are called to be cowards in the face of men. To be a coward means to make peace where there is no peace. It means to be tolerant in the face of sin and pressure. It means to proclaim peace even though the innocent and helpless are suffering.

We are not called to look away when cruelty and injustice happen. We are not called to look away when sin is revealed. We are not called to water down the truth, and we are not called to compromise. We, as Christians, are called to deal with the problems in the church and to resist this fallen world. Too many Christians are attempting to make peace with a fallen and evil world. Too many Christians are attempting to make peace within a compromised and divided church. God will judge us for declaring peace where there is no peace, especially in these last days that we are in.

"Woe to those who call evil good, and good evil; Who put darkness for light, and light for darkness; Who put bitter for sweet, and sweet for bitter!" (Isaiah 5:20, NKJV).

Jesus Himself, the Prince of Peace, was not afraid of war, nor will He be afraid of war when He returns. He did not fight in the flesh, but He fought mightily in the spirit. Do not forget, He is not just a lamb, but He is also the Lion of Judah: courageous, mighty, strong, righteous, truthful, and radical.

Jesus said this to His disciples in Matthew 10:34–37 (NKJV):

> Do not think that I came to bring peace on earth. I did not come to bring peace but a sword. For I have come to 'set a man against his father, a daughter against her mother, and a daughter-in-law against her mother-in-law'; and 'a man's enemies will be those of

his own household.' He who loves father or mother more than Me is not worthy of Me. And he who loves son or daughter more than Me is not worthy of Me.

Jesus was not bashful about the fact that the Gospel draws a clear line through humanity, society, and even family and still remains this way. Some will receive Him as their Savior, and others will reject Him. Some will stand for Him, and some will depart from Him. Others will stand with Him when it is easy, only to back down when the opposition gets too hard. We Christians must realize what the movement of the eighth horn is all about. We must see that it has already affected the church and the way many Christians think. Peace is a wonderful thing, but we cannot achieve it through compromise. We cannot go along with the compromising church. We cannot go along with the church that loves peace more than truth.

"Let's keep the peace." I cannot tell you how many times I have heard this phrase in Christian circles. This attitude has caused more harm in the body of Christ than it has done good. Instead of saying, "Let us keep the peace," we should pursue peace by speaking the truth in love and by not backing down from what is right and noble. When we speak truth in love, we love the person more than ourselves. Let us learn to ignore that uncomfortable feeling that comes when we do not conform to the easy way out.

"The wicked flee when no one pursues, But the righteous are bold as a lion" (Proverbs 28:1, NKJV).

If you want to experience true peace in your family or church, I encourage you to speak the truth in love, to stand for what is right, and to not compromise. Love the family member or church member with all your heart, but do not compromise the truth for them. Do not back down from God's design; do not turn away from God's ways. I am not ignorant of the fact that this is a completely different approach than most of us were taught in the church, but let me tell you, it is the right approach. There was not one instance in the New Testament when Jesus or the apostles compromised holiness, truth, or righteousness in order to keep peace. They knew that those Christian attributes generated true peace, so they never compromised one of them.

Even in the story about the adulteress woman, we find this truth. Jesus loved her like nobody ever had before. What she was looking for all her life, what she was looking for in that man that she slept with, she found in one instant in the presence of Jesus. His grace was sufficient for her, and He brought peace to her, but He did not compromise the truth once. He did not whitewash her sin, nor did He excuse her behavior so that she would experience a counterfeit peace. He confronted her sin so that she could find true peace on earth and peace for all of eternity by turning away from her sin.

"When Jesus had raised Himself up and saw no one but the woman, He said to her, 'Woman, where are those accusers of yours? Has no one condemned you?' She said, 'No one, Lord.' And Jesus said to her, 'Neither do I condemn you; go and sin no more'" (John 8:10–11, NKJV).

Jesus told her, "Go and sin no more" because Jesus knew that her sin would steal her peace. How often do we Christians think or feel that we have to somewhat play down the sin that reveals itself? We think that we make the other person feel too guilty by addressing it for what it is. We think that we become judgmental by addressing sin. To address sin and to call it for what it is is not being judgmental but the best and most loving thing that we can do in that moment. It is a costly thing to do, and people will dislike you and call you all kinds of things, but it is the only way to lead a person into true peace. To lovingly address sin in its entirety will open the door for full repentance. Only on the path of repentance will we find true forgiveness, and only in the depth of forgiveness will we find that beautiful peace that everyone is searching for.

The Ninth Horn—One World Order

The ninth horn's mission is to prepare for a world that is ruled by one government, a one-world order. This movement is essential for the Antichrist. Throughout all of history, nations, tribes, and cultures have warred with one another for various reasons. Material greed, strategic reasons, simply hate, or religious fanaticism were some of the leading causes of these wars. A world that consists of nations that operate in different directions would undermine the Antichrist's rule.

Based upon Daniel's vision, we know that the Antichrist is coming to have full power over the entire world and not just over several nations or regions. He craves this power, and he needs it to persecute the saints. The existence of any independent nations, especially those that are predominantly Christian, will gravely limit his reach. If nations are occupied with their own agenda, then his agenda cannot be fulfilled. Any division among nations or continents will take away from his deadly plan, so what he needs is a one-world order, one government that will rule the earth. Either he will establish this one-world order by himself when he rises to power, or he will rise to power *in* a one-world order system that was already established by the ninth horn before his coming. In whatever way this will all come to pass, I believe that the working of the ninth horn will be essential in preparing the nations for a one-world order.

Globalization and the uniting of nations began right after World War II. Since then, the world has witnessed a massive change. Borders have opened up, international opinion and standing have become more important, and economies have adjusted to serve the whole world. The uniting of the nations has never been as much in the foreground as it is today. The flagships of this global movement to connect the nations are organizations like the United Nations and the World Health Organization. We also see evidence of this in the creation of the European Union. Similar unions, like the North American Union and the African Union, exist in other parts of the world. It is loud, and it is clear what the current of this world has become. We all have been hearing the cry for open borders louder than ever before. While we still see a lot of division among the unions and alliances, it is safe to say that the world is more connected than ever before. The desire for international peace and unity is echoed by many governments around the world.

The Tenth Horn—The Great Falling Away

> Now, brethren, concerning the coming of our Lord Jesus Christ and our gathering together to Him, we ask you, not to be soon shaken in mind or troubled, either by spirit or by word or by letter, as if from us, as though the day of Christ had come. Let no one deceive you by any means; for that Day will not come unless the falling away comes first, and the man of sin is revealed, the son of perdition, who opposes and exalts himself above all that is called God or that is worshiped, so that he sits as God in the temple of God, showing himself that he is God.
>
> 2 Thessalonians 2:1–4 (NKJV)

The tenth horn is the last horn before the small horn will arise. This tenth horn is a powerful horn, and its singular focus is to shake the church. This shaking of the church is what many know as the apostasy. This immense disturbance of God's church was prophetically foretold by apostle Paul in his second letter to the church of

Thessalonica. In our Bibles, we can read about it in second Thessalonians chapter two.

Paul writes that a shaking will go through the church like nobody has ever witnessed before. I believe that we are currently in the beginning phase of this shaking. In the days and years to come, this falling away will increase dramatically. Everything in the church that is not founded on the Rock will fall away. Only the very branches that are firmly connected to the Vine will remain. Our heavenly Father, who desires to see a pure church that is built firmly on the Rock, will allow this shaking to happen. He desires to see Christians who are personally connected to His Son and who do not seek a connection to this fallen world. Those who are connected to the fallen concepts of humanity will fall with them, but those who have been renewed in their thinking through the power of the Holy Spirit will stand resolute in these trying days. Those with loyal and soft hearts of love will remain flexible and connected to Jesus and His body throughout the periods of the utmost shaking. Anyone who is connected to the fallen world will fall with this world, but those who are connected to Jesus will stand firm with Him for all eternity.

> See that you do not refuse Him who speaks. For if they did not escape who refused Him who spoke on earth, much more shall we not escape if we turn away from Him who speaks from heaven, whose voice then shook the earth; but now He has promised, saying, "Yet once more I shake not only the earth, but also heaven." Now this, "Yet once more," indicates the removal of those things that are being shaken, as of things that are made, that the things which cannot be shaken may remain.
>
> Therefore, since we are receiving a kingdom which

cannot be shaken, let us have grace, by which we may serve God acceptably with reverence and godly fear. For our God is a consuming fire.

Hebrews 12:25–29 (NKJV)

The apostasy is called "the great falling away" because a large part of the church will actually fall away from God. Deception, a lack of truth, lukewarmness, earthly pleasures, earthly riches, and earthly fame will be some of the chief reasons for this great departure from God. If we dare to open our eyes, we already see the beginning of this great departure from God in the societies of this world. In America, we see this falling away at an alarming rate as people try ruthlessly to get rid of God in our schools, in the media, and in our government. But not only in the secular world do we see the signs of the great departure; in more and more churches, we hear the preaching of another Jesus. A Jesus who is all about giving us a nice and comfortable life, a Jesus who is there to fulfill our dreams and our visions, a Jesus who is fine with us being silent and inactive about Him, a Jesus who tickles our ears and whose purpose is to forgive our sins without ever changing our heart. Millions of Christians come daily to the throne of grace to find forgiveness and freedom from guilt, but they never receive or ask for grace to live pure lives. Millions of Christians are being taught a lukewarm Gospel, a Gospel that lacks surrender, holiness, the fear of God, and the call of repentance that leads us to His cross. The ones who have not heard the full Gospel of Christ, the ones who have not been engulfed with His love and filled with His Spirit, will not stand on solid ground when the shaking intensifies. The feel-good Gospel that they have heard, received, and lived out will contradict the lifestyle that is required to endure the shaking of all things. Needed attributes like endurance, perseverance, self-sacrifice, sacrificial love, unshakable faith, and absolute commitment to Him will be foreign to the ones who have lived out the diluted Gospel, which will result in a great falling away. It will be *the* "when the rubber hits the road" moment for the church, and many will sadly reject the way that leads to the true Jesus.

I believe that this falling away will be the final signal of the imminent arrival of the Antichrist. Right after Paul talks about the great falling away, he begins to talk about the final Antichrist. In the famous second chapter of second Thessalonians, he calls the Antichrist *the man of sin, the son of perdition,* and *the lawless one.*

> Let no one deceive you by any means; for that Day will not come unless the falling away comes first, and the man of sin is revealed, the son of perdition, who opposes and exalts himself above all that is called God or that is worshiped, so that he sits as God in the temple of God, showing himself that he is God.
>
> Do you not remember that when I was still with you I told you these things? And now you know what is restraining, that he may be revealed in his own time. For the mystery of lawlessness is already at work; only He who now restrains will do so until He is taken out of the way. And then the lawless one will be revealed, whom the Lord will consume with the breath of His mouth and destroy with the brightness of His coming. The coming of the lawless one is according to the working of Satan, with all power, signs, and lying wonders, and with all unrighteous deception among those who perish, because they did not receive the love of the truth, that they might be saved. And for this reason God will send them strong delusion, that they should believe the lie, that they all

may be condemned who did not believe the truth but had pleasure in unrighteousness.

2 Thessalonians 2:3–12 (NKJV)

Can you see that the mystery of lawlessness is already at work all over the world and that this lawlessness has been hitting the shores of America with great force for decades? Satan is eagerly working to make this world more and more lawless. He is using the tenth horn to prepare this world for the coming of the lawless one, the Antichrist.

"The coming of the lawless one is according to the working of Satan, with all power, signs, and lying wonders, and with all unrighteous deception among those who perish, because they did not receive the love of the truth, that they might be saved" (2 Thessalonians 2:9–10, NKJV).

What is lawlessness? It is the state of disorder due to a complete disregard of the law.

It is very important that we understand how this state of disorder and this disregard of the law will look when the lawless one comes. Some might think that when the Antichrist appears, the world will be in complete disorder, chaos, anarchy, and without any system of law, but I don't believe that this will be the case. On the contrary, there will be complete order and there will be strict laws in place that will be established by the world government under the Antichrist's rule. So why, then, does the Bible call him the lawless one?

In the eyes of the fallen world, the Antichrist will not look like a lawless ruler. That's why Paul called it the *mystery of lawlessness*. It will be a mystery to the world; it will be undetected and hidden from this world. This world will be absolutely oblivious to the lawlessness that the Antichrist will bring as they will live in strong delusion and as they will not have a love for the truth.

> And with all unrighteous deception among those who perish, because they did not receive the love of the truth, that they might be saved. And for this reason God will send them strong delusion, that they should believe the lie, that they all may be condemned who did not believe the truth but had pleasure in unrighteousness.
>
> 2 Thessalonians 2:10–12 (NKJV)

The state of disorder will not be seen in the natural realm, but it will be seen in the spiritual realm. The lawlessness will be according to God's view and not the view of this fallen world. There will not be a disregard for worldly law and order but for God's law and His order. Laws will be set into place that will completely contradict God's law. These laws will be heralded as laws of freedom, laws of integration, laws of diversity, and laws of human rights by the world, but in God's eyes, these laws will bring great lawlessness. People will be released to commit murder, live out idolatry, enjoy perversions, and participate in many other evil acts under these world laws while, according to God's law, they are committing great and grievous sins. What we have already witnessed with abortion laws and laws of sexual freedom will grow and increase in the years ahead. This world will become an environment in which the lawless one will feel at home and in which true Christians will be seen as criminals and vagabonds. Any Christian that has been spiritually awake has noticed this increase in lawlessness and any Christian that has not noticed this increase has some catching up to do.

— RIGHT BEFORE OUR EYES —

Recently, my family and I traveled to Europe to celebrate my brother's wedding. In preparation for the wedding, my brother and I had a haircut appointment in the middle of Amsterdam. The city was very crowded, traffic was everywhere, and we had a hard time finding a parking spot. After a lot of driving around and searching, we finally found a parking spot where I could park my rental car. Shortly after exiting my car, I realized we had parked right in front of a brothel. On the other side of each of the big windows sat or stood a prostitute with very little clothing. These women were displayed like any other merchandise a person would look at when shopping. This brothel was not out of sight on the outskirts of town but right in the busy center filled with people, tourists, and families. And no one seemed to care. We quickly left the area and finally made it to a famous open-air market where my brother wanted to buy some olives and cheese for his wedding reception. After about five minutes at this market, our pleasant shopping experience was harshly interrupted as we heard troubling screaming just around the corner from us. We suddenly witnessed a big commotion among the people at this market, and my brother and I ran toward the source of the noise and screaming. After a few steps, we realized what had happened. A man high on drugs had thrown himself out of a third-story window. He was lying lifeless and drenched in blood on the cobblestone of this famous market street. As I watched my brother kneeling down next to this man and praying for him, I noticed a second person appearing at the window from where this man had thrown himself. I had seen brutal carnage before while traveling as a missionary in Africa, and what I saw on the ground in front of me was indeed very disturbing. Far more disturbing to me, however, was seeing the face of the man standing at the window above us. His face was pale, and his eyes were wide open, staring down at his friend, who was lying lifeless on the cobblestone. What I saw on this man's face was an absolute shock, death, and hopelessness. It was like looking at someone who just had an audience with the devil himself. I will never forget this man's lifeless expression. The police and paramedics showed up quickly, and my brother and I began walking back to our car. On the way back, I knew what I had just witnessed—from the brothel where women were displayed as merchandise to the man who had thrown himself out of a window in his delirium—had happened because of the growing lawlessness in this world. Prostitution and drug culture are prominent in cities like Amsterdam because the laws of men make these cultures flourish.

What I witnessed in half an hour in Amsterdam is what is coming for the rest of the world. It is the current of the tenth horn that is coming hard against any godly law and principle. It is the current that is coming against America with force. And it is a current that can only be held back with true revival.

— CHAPTER 13: —
THE THREE STEPS OF THE ANTICHRIST

THREE MUST BE SUBDUED

"The ten horns are ten kings who shall arise from this kingdom. And another shall rise after them; He shall be different from the first ones, and shall subdue three kings" (Daniel 7:24, NKJV).

From these verses, we get some very important information: the ten horns are ten kings, and out of the ten kings, three will be subdued by the small horn, the Antichrist. This means that once all the movements of the ten horns are complete, once the ten horns have achieved what they came to achieve, the Antichrist will arise and subdue three of them. I believe that those three kings are the first three horns that I have mentioned in the previous chapter.

Without subduing the first three kings, the Antichrist will not be able to sit on the throne that he so desperately needs. "To subdue" means "to bring something under control." Now, you may wonder why the Antichrist would subdue three of the ten horns that previously prepared the way for him. Why would Antichrist subdue his own helpers? To find out why, we must go back and look at what the first three horns are all about.

The first horn is the movement of "counterfeit religion." The second horn is the movement of "humanism," and the third horn is the movement of "counterfeit ideology." All three movements have one thing in common: they offer a counterfeit way for humanity. It is the wide and crooked way beside the narrow way that Jesus offers to all mankind. All three of them offer another way to compete with the only way that leads to salvation. They use stark distraction, intentional brainwashing, and subtle deception to pull millions and even billions of people away from Jesus. Instead of offering the way, the truth, and the life, these three horns offered a way paved with lies that would ultimately lead to death.

While the spirit of Antichrist fully intended for the three horns to fulfill their purpose of deceiving billions of people, all three movements must come under the control of the final Antichrist in order for him to rule over the entire world. You may wonder why.

All three movements are, at their cores, extremely fanatic, aggressive, and not united. Unlike the other seven movements, the three first three horns have more power and potency. The followers of each of these movements are so fanatic that they will oppose each other to the death. These movements are so extreme that they will never be united under the rule of the Antichrist. He knows that a house that is divided against itself cannot stand, and for that reason, he must subdue them and bring them under his control.

Think about it: the philosopher who is under the power of humanism and who believes in pagan gods will always insult the Muslim who is under the power of counterfeit religion. The atheist Communist who is under the power of counterfeit ideology will always collide with the devoted Hindu under the power of counterfeit religion. The nationalist who is under the power of counterfeit ideology will always infuriate the freethinking philosopher who is under the power of humanism. Even within each of the three movements, there are too many extremes for the Antichrist to unite them. The nationalist disagrees with the globalist-thinking Communists, and the Muslims will cause offense to the other counterfeit religions.

For the Antichrist to rule over all the world and for him to have the power that he needs in order to persecute the saints, counterfeit religion, counterfeit ideology, and humanism must come under his control. He must subdue the first three kings to become the king of the world.

I am not entirely sure how the Antichrist will achieve this, but it is a move that will and must happen in order for him to rule over all the earth. We must remember that behind each of these three movements are powerful spirits. Otherwise, they would not be able to deceive billions of people. However, according to the hierarchy of the kingdom of darkness, the Antichrist has more authority and power than any of those spirits, as he is empowered by the strongest spirit, the spirit of Antichrist. It is entirely possible that his power will be so strong that the fanatics of these movements will simply drop everything they have formerly believed and follow him instantly. They already have been deceived once by each of the three horns, so what would prevent them from being deceived by the greater force of the Antichrist?

It is also entirely possible that the Antichrist will somehow unite those three movements and that they will come together under his lead, as all three movements are at their very core against Christianity. Unlike Christians, the followers of the three kings do not have the truth of the written Word, nor do they have the Holy Spirit as a counselor and guide. They are living in absolute darkness. They are like little children lost in a deep, dark forest. There is no truth in the books of their man-made religion and ideology. There is no truth in those books that they feed upon daily, so when the day of the Antichrist comes, they will be like hopeless prey.

The Bible tells us to take heed that we are not deceived. Think about that. We have the written Word that is jam-packed with truth, and we know the precious Holy Spirit who always desires to guide us into all truth. Even though we have been set on such a firm foundation by our heavenly Father, He still warns us to take heed that we are not deceived. He warns us because He knows how deceptive and cunning the kingdom of darkness is. Imagine being a follower of one of the three horns and having to go through those days without any foundation. They will get swiftly snatched up, and they will be utterly lost.

As I said earlier, the followers of the first three movements are fanatics. One problem with fanatics is that they live an unbalanced life. They are not just affected by some strange doctrine or ideology, but they are actually driven by it. A fanatic has an unbalanced craving for signs and wonders. I believe that the Antichrist will use this open door in the lives of those fanatics to subdue them. He will not just be a man of deceptive and cunning words, but he will be a man of lying signs and wonders. Let's go back one more time to that powerful scripture in second Thessalonians as it talks about exactly this. It talks about the people who have been deceived by these movements, and it talks about how the Antichrist will deceive them to follow him.

> The coming of the lawless one is according to the working of Satan, with all power, signs, and lying wonders, and with all unrighteous deception among those who perish, because they did not receive the love of the truth, that they might be saved. And for this reason God will send them strong delusion, that they should believe the lie.
>
> 2 Thessalonians 2:9–11 (NKJV)

These are the three ways the Antichrist could use to subdue the followers of the three horns:

1. His power and authority will subdue the spirits behind the three horns, and the followers will naturally flock to him.

2. He will subdue them by uniting them under the purpose of persecuting all true Christians. The truth that Christians carry goes exactly against what the followers of the three horns believe. The truth in us kindles their hatred toward us Christians today, but even more so when the Antichrist will rule.

3. He will use lying signs and wonders to convince them that he is superior to their gods and movements, and in return, they will flock to him.

— CHAPTER 14: —
THE SMALL HORN

WHY IS THE LAST HORN SMALL?

The Antichrist is described as a powerful individual, so powerful indeed that he will be able to subdue the first three horns. He will be exceedingly strong, so strong that he will rule over the entire world and kill many Christians. How is it, then, that Daniel's vision describes him as the small horn?

One of the devil's tactics is to disguise himself. When he tricked Eve into eating the forbidden fruit, he did so in disguise. He appeared to her as a snake instead of his fallen nature. The Antichrist will follow the same playbook. The horn in Daniel's vision is described as small, not in reference to the Antichrist's power, nor in reference to his might, but in reference to his disguise. He will come as a small horn because it is the perfect camouflage and fits his deceptive nature. When he comes on the scene, he will appear innocent, like a wolf in sheep's clothing. He will offer counterfeit peace, he will bring counterfeit unity, and under those two counterfeits, he will bring the whole world together. Every nation, every tribe, every fringe group, will not see him in his true nature but in disguise. He will lure everyone in, just as Absalom stole Israel's heart when he was waiting at King David's gate. All of humanity will fall for the small horn except the ones who love Jesus unto death and are guided by the Spirit of truth. The Antichrist will appear like a savior, he will tickle people's ears, and he will accept the world in its sins without giving it an antidote for its sins. Sin will be accepted and celebrated, and multitudes will flock to him.

The Antichrist is the small horn because he will fit perfectly into the picture that the ten horns will have painted. The colors that the ten horns have applied will cover his evil nature. He will be an artist just like Adolf Hitler and Emperor Nero were artists, full of themselves and worshiped by men. That is the very nature of Satan, and it will be lived out by the Antichrist. Lucifer was a beautiful angel in charge of worship. Lucifer was an artist. He became prideful and full of himself and began worshiping himself. He stirred up other angels and successfully stole a portion of worship that was only intended for the One true God. This nature of Satan will shine through the Antichrist, and the rebellious world will receive him. He will receive the worship of men, and the Antichrist will invite them into eternal death and destruction by worshiping himself. He will deceive humanity because he will not appear violent but innocent, not evil but caring, not of darkness but of light.

"And no wonder! For Satan himself transforms himself into an angel of light" (2 Corinthians 11:14, NKJV).

A MAN—A SMALL HORN—A COUNTERFEIT JESUS

One of the most deceiving attributes about the Antichrist is that he will come as a man and a counterfeit Christ. He will come as a man, just like Jesus did. Jesus came as the Son of God, lived a perfect life to save humanity, and was rejected. The Antichrist will come as a son of lies and will live a sinful life, yet he will be received by a sinful world. He will be a counterfeit Christ, not offering a way to be free of sin but whitewashing the sin of the world to lead them into eternal damnation. This small horn's appearance, his embracing of sin, and his coming as a man will fool many.

In chapter thirteen of the book of Revelation, we find John's vision about the Antichrist. At the end of the vision, we read these important words that confirm that the Antichrist will come to the world as a man:

"Here is wisdom. Let him who has understanding calculate the number of the beast, for it is the number of a man: His number is 666" (Revelation 13:18, NKJV).

THE SPREADING OF THE GOSPEL CEASES

Only the Father knows the day of His Son's return, and only the Father knows exactly when the Antichrist will rise to power. Based on scripture, however, we receive insights about the spiritual climate the world will be in when the Antichrist will claim his throne.

In history, every time the spirit of Antichrist rose up, God pushed it back, reminding it that this world is not running on the devil's timing but on God's timing. He was reminding that spirit who is truly in charge. Only when every nation and every tribe has heard the Gospel, only when the Gospel has bounced off the ends of this world, will the Antichrist be permitted to come.

"And He said to them, 'Go into all the world and preach the gospel to every creature. He who believes and is baptized will be saved; but he who does not believe will be condemned'" (Mark 16:15–16, NKJV).

"And this gospel of the kingdom will be preached in all the world as a witness to all the nations, and then the end will come" (Matthew 24:14, NKJV).

CHAPTER 15:
THE END-TIME BRIDE

ENDURING TRIALS

There is a lot of speculation and theories out there in regard to the tribulation and the rapture. Some say Jesus will rapture us before the tribulation, some say He will rapture us in the middle of the tribulation, and some say He will rapture us at the end of the tribulation. I am going to be honest; I do not want to get into that topic in this book. What I want to focus on is something similar but yet different. There is an important question to be asked and an important answer to be given. The question is: *will Christians still be on earth when the Antichrist will rule?*

We might not like this question, and we might not even like to think about it, but I believe that we, as believers, must be aware of what the Bible says in regard to this. Many Christians seem to ignore this question, and many people actually think that we will not be here for the Antichrist's rule. I would love to believe that too, but I cannot ignore how clear scripture is about this question. Instead of running away from this question, I believe that we must be prepared for what is coming. Daniel's vision couldn't be clearer about this question:

> I was watching; and the same horn was making war against the saints, and prevailing against them, until

> the Ancient of Days came, and a judgment was made in favor of the saints of the Most High, and the time came for the saints to possess the kingdom.
>
> Daniel 7:21–22 (NKJV)

"He shall speak pompous words against the Most High, shall persecute the saints of the Most High, and shall intend to change times and law. Then the saints shall be given into his hand for a time and times and half a time" (Daniel 7:25, NKJV).

Not only does Daniel's end-time vision tell us that the Christians will be on earth during the Antichrist's rule, but John's end-time vision makes this abundantly clear as well.

> And he was given a mouth speaking great things and blasphemies, and he was given authority to continue for forty-two months. Then he opened his mouth in blasphemy against God, to blaspheme His name, His tabernacle, and those who dwell in heaven. It was granted to him to make war with the saints and to overcome them. And authority was given him over every tribe, tongue, and nation. All who dwell on the earth will worship him, whose names have not been written in the Book of Life of the Lamb slain from the foundation of the world.
>
> Revelation 13:5–8 (NKJV)

Based on Daniel's and John's vision, it could not be clearer that we Christians will have to endure the persecution of the Antichrist. I am aware that this knowledge might cause worry or fear to arise in our hearts. I am aware that some might be terrified by the thought of being persecuted and killed for their faith. Some might wonder even why our heavenly Father would allow such pain among us, the people who love Him. Allow me to answer those concerns, worries, and questions.

First and foremost, I want to say this: remember who our God is.

He has promised us that He will never forsake us nor leave us, no matter how dark it gets. We must trust Him and trust that if He has decided for the Christians to endure the persecution of the Antichrist, He also knows what He is doing. If it is the Lord's will for us believers to be on earth when the Antichrist rules, then we also know that God will give us what we need in those days. God is a promise keeper, and His Word says that His grace will be sufficient for us no matter what may come. Let us focus on that promise. Whatever we will face today or in the future, we must remember that His grace will be enough. The Bible does not tell us that His grace will only be enough in the good times but that His grace also will be enough in the darkest days that we will ever face. Yes, Christians will be killed for their faith in Jesus, but the Antichrist will only be able to kill the body. The moment that they give up their ghost, they will wake up in the loving arms of Jesus Christ.

Knowing that His grace will be sufficient in those dark days, I now want to focus on answering two questions that people have asked in regard to this:

1. Why do we, as Christians, have to endure the persecution of the Antichrist?

2. Why would Jesus not snatch us away before?

It is important to know the answer to these two questions so that the devil cannot use a lack of knowledge on our part to defeat us in those days. He will always try to separate us from God, so understanding God's plan in those days is very essential. Knowing the answers to those two questions will not only give us the necessary fuel to endure but also protection from receiving the devil's deadly seeds of doubt.

THE PURIFICATION OF THE BRIDE

"Let us be glad and rejoice and give Him glory, for the marriage of the Lamb has come, and His wife has made herself ready" (Revelation 19:7, NKJV).

There are many scriptures in the Bible that speak about endurance, perseverance, patience, and purification. Many of those are made in context to the end times. Before we focus on the part that we have to play in the last days, I want to emphasize that it is Jesus who has prepared a way into the holiest of holies for us. It is Jesus that has torn the veil, and only by His blood are we redeemed. There is no other way to the Father but through Jesus. We are saved by grace and not by our works. No matter how zealous and no matter how determined we are, we can never make up for Christ's all-sufficient sacrifice. Without Him, we can never become a bride without spots, wrinkles, or blemishes.

> Husbands, love your wives, just as Christ also loved the church and gave Himself for her, that He might sanctify and cleanse her with the washing of water by the word, that He might present her to Himself a glorious church, not having spot or wrinkle or any such thing, but that she should be holy and without blemish.
>
> Ephesians 5:25–27 (NKJV)

Now, with this truth being established, we must also know that we all have a part in the preparation of the bride. After all, we are the bride. There is a choice on our end that is required today and there is a choice required for the church of the last days, which very likely could be us. It is an important choice to allow the Father to purify us. You and I cannot purify ourselves, nor can we change ourselves. All we can do is to allow Jesus to purify us. A person who is loyal to the Bridegroom is a person who has a heart that desires purification, a heart that is willing to receive the Father's chastening. The chastening of our heavenly Father will always produce purity in our lives and a closer intimacy between us and His Son. Only those who truly love Jesus will endure the Father's chastening, and only those who truly know the Father will understand His chastening.

> I am jealous for you with a godly jealousy. I promised you to one husband, to Christ, so that I might present you as a pure virgin to him. But I am afraid that just as Eve was deceived by the serpent's cunning, your minds may somehow be led astray from your sincere and pure devotion to Christ.
>
> 2 Corinthians 11:2–3 (NIV)

All persecution, all trials, and all tribulation are allowed by our heavenly Father so that when His Son Jesus returns, He will be embraced by a pure bride. A pure virgin bride has not known any other man, just like Christ's bride has no other gods or idols. She has made the decision to be set apart for her Bridegroom. She patiently waits for the special day of her marriage and covenant. A pure bride will forsake her standing in society, her wealth, her parents, and her family to start a new life with her Bridegroom. That is the life that we committed to when we made Jesus our Lord and Savior. Right now, we are that bride, betrothed to Jesus, and our marriage will only happen if we truly desire to forsake everything else to marry the Bridegroom.

To be married to His Son Jesus is what the Father truly desires for all of us. This calling of the end-time bride is like the calling that was on Esther's life. Just like she was purified before meeting the king, we must be purified before marrying our heavenly King. Esther went through a rigorous purifying process; she was willing to endure this process, and God's favor was upon her.

The Father will not allow a bride that will make His precious Son wait. He will not allow a lukewarm bride, nor will He allow a bride that will cause His Son shame. Jesus endured all of the shame of humanity once and for all when He was hanging on that rugged cross: He will not endure shame on His wedding day. He carried our sin and shame as an innocent Lamb. The Lamb carried our shame and sin, but not the Lion of Judah. We must never forget that Jesus came as a Lamb, but He will return as a glorious Lion. He came as an innocent Lamb so that we can stand in righteousness when He returns as a Lion. If we neglect to cast our sin, shame, and guilt upon the Lamb, then we will not be ready when the Lion returns. The nature of the Lamb is humble and meek, but the Lion embodies judgment and righteousness. The Lamb is the prey, while the Lion is the predator. Only those who are marked by the blood of the Lamb will not become the prey of the Lion of Judah. The blood of the Lamb is for those who love and cherish the Lamb, it is for those who lost their life for the Lamb, and it is for those who prepared themselves for the Lion.

It is important for all of us to understand that the Father did not hold anything back from us when He sent His only begotten Son. In the same spirit, we must not hold anything back from Him until Christ returns. For this very reason, will the Father allow the Antichrist to persecute the believers because the persecution that the saints will have to endure will be the final stage of purification for Christ's bride. Persecution always has been and always will be the ultimate test of the Christian life. It tests the intentions of the heart like nothing else will. To be willing to die for someone means to love them more than life itself.

Jesus made this very clear in Matthew 16:24–25 (NKJV): "Then Jesus said to His disciples, 'If anyone desires to come after Me, let him deny himself, and take up his cross, and follow Me. For whoever desires to save his life will lose it, but whoever loses his life for My sake will find it.'"

Think about the disciples. It is clear that Jesus absolutely loved them, yet out of the twelve apostles, eleven died for Christ. Should the Christians of the last days expect a different outcome? The truth is that today's church has mostly rejected persecution. We are used to hearing about it in faraway African and Asian countries, but what if there would be persecution here in America? Would as many people claim to be Christians? Would as many people go to church on Sunday if it could cost us our lives? We believe in Jesus, but do we believe in Him unto death? Many pursue the comfortable Christian life but not the radical Christian life. Today's Western church is not ready to face persecution, which ultimately reveals a sad truth. Today's church is not ready to meet the Bridegroom. If we are not willing to endure persecution for the One who we gave our lives, can He be really on the throne of our hearts? Can He really inherit the rightful place of Savior, Lord, and Bridegroom?

HOW TO ENDURE THE RULE OF THE ANTICHRIST

In the book of Revelation, we read about how we can overcome the devil, the Antichrist, and all powers of darkness.

"And they overcame him by the blood of the Lamb and by the word of their testimony, and they did not love their lives to the death" (Revelation 12:11, NKJV).

There are *three important keys* in this scripture:

1. The true church will overcome the devil by the wonder-working blood of Jesus.

2. The true Christians will overcome the devil by their powerful testimony of Christ's redemption.

3. The true Christians will overcome the devil by loving Jesus more than their own natural lives and the fear of death.

When quoting this strategical verse, many people leave out the last part of this verse. It is important to state that we cannot overcome the accuser by Jesus' blood and our testimony alone. The key to overcoming the devil and the trials of the last days is made up of three equal parts: the blood of Jesus, our testimony of salvation, and loving Jesus more than our own natural lives. We must love Him more than the fear of physical death. These three points in Revelation 12:11 form a powerful key that will open every prison door of the kingdom of darkness. Persecution is the fiery furnace that tests this powerful three-pronged key in our lives. It is our response to persecution that will make or break this key. Persecution is our final test, just as the cross was the final act of obedience and absolute surrender for Jesus. He asked the Father if there was any way that the cup could pass Him by, but there was no way around it. He then willingly and obediently laid down His life so that you and I could find eternal life. We must do the same in the face of persecution: lay down our lives to seal our eternal life.

Jesus Himself told us about these days of persecution, yet somehow, we don't talk about it in the Western church. He talks about the same persecution that Daniel saw in his vision.

> Then they will deliver you up to tribulation and kill you, and you will be hated by all nations for My

name's sake. And then many will be offended, will betray one another, and will hate one another. Then many false prophets will rise up and deceive many. And because lawlessness will abound, the love of many will grow cold. But he who endures to the end shall be saved.

> Matthew 24:9–13 (NKJV)

These will not be easy times for the church. But I believe that in those times, Jesus will be even closer to His soon-to-be bride. Even though Christians will be delivered up to death, even though we will be hated by all nations, and even though many Christians will betray each other to escape the deadly persecution, Jesus will be very near to us. Hallelujah!

> And pray that your flight may not be in winter or on the Sabbath. For then there will be great tribulation, such as has not been since the beginning of the world until this time, no, nor ever shall be. And unless those days were shortened, no flesh would be saved; but for the elect's sake those days will be shortened.

> Matthew 24:20–22 (NKJV)

The Father's heart is for all of us to come through those perilous times of persecution and tribulation. We learn in these verses that in His mercy, the Father will shorten those days of persecution so that His very elected bride will make it through. Do you remember the passage in Daniel when it said that the Antichrist would try to change times and laws?

I believe that the attempt of the Antichrist to change times and laws means that the Antichrist's intention is to lengthen the days of persecution so that more Christians will walk away from Jesus, the Bridegroom, before His coming. In His mercy and love for the bride, however, the Father will not allow the Antichrist to prolong this season but will actually cut it short so that His very elect will make it.

Let me ask you, where are you at with all of this? Can you see how the scriptures are clear about this? And are you willing to die and lose everything for Jesus? These are sobering questions, and I encourage you not to run from these questions but to embrace them wholeheartedly. Now is the time to prepare our hearts. Now is the time to know the answer to those questions, and now is the time to make a commitment to Jesus that will last through every storm, every trial, and even the persecution of the last days.

DO NOT FEAR

"As soon as Jesus heard the word that was spoken, He said to the ruler of the synagogue, 'Do not be afraid; only believe'" (Mark 5:36, NKJV).

My friend Winfried Wentland and his wife, Gaby, have lived their lives by these six words found in Mark 5:36 (NKJV): *"Do not be afraid; only believe."* For forty years, they have put themselves in the line of fire for the sake of the Gospel. They chose not to be afraid but instead to believe in Jesus in all situations. From being in the most dangerous situations and places while preaching the Gospel in Africa to rescuing women from vicious sex traffickers, Winfried and Gaby have shown me, my family, and many others what it means to not be afraid and to simply trust in Jesus. I highly recommend you to read their book *By Life or by Death*. It's a testament to two people who decided not to be moved by fear but by love and faith instead, placing themselves into dangerous and deadly situations time and time again, but instead of experiencing death, they only found life beyond the boundary of fear.

We all can come to that place through the love of Jesus and by choosing to trust Him. I myself had the privilege to work for Winfried for two years and witnessed firsthand his fearless attitude. Thanks to him, and obviously, thanks to Jesus, it is now something I have grown in. It is something I believe we all must grow in when facing the end times. Fear is a liar and a thief, and it will keep a person from fulfilling their calling and destiny in Christ if we allow it. Are you not tired of being moved by fear instead of love? Are you not tired of being moved by the "what-ifs" instead of faith? If so, it is time to slay that giant of fear, and God has given us a mighty weapon to do so. That weapon is called love.

"For God has not given us a spirit of fear, but of power and of love and of a sound mind" (2 Timothy 1:7, NKJV).

It is only His love that will enable us to endure those days. It is only His love that will allow us to make a commitment to Him. He loved us first so that we can love Him in return. If you are fearful about the days to come, chances are that you are already experiencing fear in your everyday life.

If you experience fear in your daily walk and if you have fear about what is coming, then you must reach out for the love of Jesus. You desperately need it. Without His love, we always become fearful, and fear always leads to torment. When we receive a full dose of the love of the Bridegroom, we are liberated from any fear. Ask Him right now to fill you with His love. Ask Him to move away all the stones in your heart and to make it soft. Ask Him for a taste of His love every morning. Each day, we must experience His love in order to love Him and the people in our lives.

"There is no fear in love; but perfect love casts out fear, because fear involves torment. But he who fears has not been made perfect in love" (1 John 4:18, NKJV).

Once you have received His love you then have to make the most loving decision a person can make. Trust Him. Trusting another person can only be done in love. Full trust is only found in the depth of pure love. Once you receive the love of Jesus, you must make the decision to trust Him with your life, your family, and your future. Place yourself fully into His hands every day afresh, and you will find that as your love and trust grow, fear declines until it is no more. In that place of full trust and love, you will then experience true freedom. Nothing and no one will be able to hold you back from your destiny any longer, but you will be fully ruled by love, and you will join Jesus' company of burning hearts.

"Trust in the Lord with all your heart, And lean not on your own understanding; In all your ways acknowledge Him, And He shall direct your paths" (Proverbs 3:5–6, NKJV).

— CHAPTER 16: —
JOHN'S IDENTICAL VISION

In the previous two chapters, I referred to two scriptures from chapter thirteen in the book of Revelation. In this chapter, we read about a powerful vision that John received about the Antichrist. In the closing of this book, I felt it very important to have a look at John's vision as it not only confirms Daniel's vision but gives us extra details that Daniel's vision did not cover.

> Then I stood on the sand of the sea. And I saw a beast rising up out of the sea, having seven heads and ten horns, and on his horns ten crowns, and on his heads a blasphemous name. Now the beast which I saw was like a leopard, his feet were like the feet of a bear, and his mouth like the mouth of a lion.
>
> Revelation 13:1–2 (NKJV)

Just like in Daniel's vision, John's vision describes how the beast comes out of the sea. While Daniel's vision describes it as separate beasts, John's vision describes It as one beast with different parts. The beast in John's vision has seven heads with ten horns and crowns. The ten horns and the ten crowns in John's vision line up with Daniel's vision, but how do the seven heads line up with Daniel's vision?

Amazingly, the seven heads line up as well. If you go through the beasts in Daniel's vision and count the heads of every beast, you end up with seven heads. The lion with the eagle's wings had one head, the bear had one head, the leopard had four heads, and the last beast had one head with ten horns and ten crowns. John continues to then describe the beast, and it goes without saying that he is describing the same beast. The beast that came out of the great sea was like a leopard with the feet of a bear and the mouth of a lion. On top of the leopard's head were ten horns and ten crowns. Can you see how John's vision is talking about the same things as Daniel's vision?

Let us look closely at the rest of John's vision and let us look at other similarities between the two visions. Also, allow me to point out some new and important details about the Antichrist that we do not find in Daniel's vision.

ONE HEAD WAS MORTALLY WOUNDED

In Revelation 13:2–4 (NKJV), we read,

> The dragon gave him his power, his throne, and great authority. And I saw one of his heads as if it had been mortally wounded, and his deadly wound was healed. And all the world marveled and followed the beast. So they worshiped the dragon who gave authority to the beast; and they worshiped the beast, saying, "Who is like the beast? Who is able to make war with him?"

John's vision does not undermine Daniel's vision, but it confirms it and gives us important additional details. To start, one thing about John's vision is that the four beasts appear as one beast with different features and seven heads, while in Daniel's vision, the four beasts are described more by their connection to each other. As we read verses 2–4, we learn that one of the seven heads will get mortally wounded and that the wound will get healed. In response, the world will follow and worship the beast and worship the dragon, who gave the beast power.

I believe that the one head out of the seven heads that will get wounded represents the fourth beast and, ultimately, the final Antichrist. This lines up perfectly with Daniel's vision. The very fact that John's vision describes only one beast with different features and seven heads reveals to us the unity among the four beasts. Daniel's vision showed us a connection between the four beasts but not such unity. I believe that John's vision gives us an important revelation that was not emphasized in Daniel's vision. It shows that all four beasts really had one common mission: to establish the kingdom of the Antichrist and to create a world in which the dragon would be worshiped. It also reveals that the spirit of Antichrist was behind every single beast of Daniel's vision.

You may wonder, who is the dragon? The devil is the dragon. Revelation 12:9 (NKJV) makes this abundantly clear: "So the great dragon was cast out, that serpent of old, called the Devil and Satan, who deceives the whole world; he was cast to the earth, and his angels were cast out with him."

The statement that the dragon (the devil) gave authority to the beast confirms the working of the spirit of Antichrist among the beast, or the fourth beast, as highlighted earlier in this book.

"And I saw one of his heads as if it had been mortally wounded, and his deadly wound was healed. And all the world marveled and followed the beast" (Revelation 13:3, NKJV).

Both Daniel's and John's visions reveal that the Antichrist will come as a man, as a small horn, to deceive humanity into following him. What does verse 3 mean?

This could mean that there will be an assassination attempt on the Antichrist and that he will be miraculously healed. The devil could use the advancements of today's technology and the power of social media to then share the assassination attempt and the healing of the wound with the whole world. In response, the world would receive the man, the Antichrist, and make him its leader. A world that has been suspicious of every move of God would then have a reason not to believe in God because the Antichrist will not give glory to God for the healing but to himself and the dragon. Once again, it becomes abundantly clear that the devil cannot create but can only come up with counterfeits. He will try to copy Jesus' death and resurrection by allowing the Antichrist to be mortally wounded and then healed. Billions will fall for it and receive the Antichrist.

"And all the world marveled and followed the beast" (Revelation 13:3, NKJV*)*.

"So they worshiped the dragon who gave authority to the beast; and they worshiped the beast, saying, 'Who is like the beast? Who is able to make war with him?'" (Revelation 13:4, NKJV).

Look at the effects of this possible scenario. Just as it was stated in Daniel's vision, the Antichrist will rule over the whole world, steal the worship of men, and blaspheme God.

THE ANTICHRIST'S RULE ACCORDING TO JOHN'S VISION

"And he was given a mouth speaking great things and blasphemies, and he was given authority to continue for forty-two months. Then he opened his mouth in blasphemy against God, to blaspheme His name, His tabernacle, and those who dwell in heaven" (Revelation 13:5–6, NKJV).

Do you remember how long the Antichrist will rule according

to Daniel's vision? In Daniel's vision, he ruled for a time, times, and half a time, which collates to three and a half years. How many months are in three and a half years? Forty-two months. This is another confirmation that John's and Daniel's visions speak about the same thing.

THE SAME MISSION

"It was granted to him to make war with the saints and to overcome them. And authority was given him over every tribe, tongue, and nation" (Revelation 13:7, NKJV).

Just as described in Daniel's vision, John's vision also states that the Antichrist will be permitted to persecute the saints. There will be no safe nation or territory since he will have authority over the whole earth. Daniel said that the Antichrist will devour the whole earth, while John wrote down that the Antichrist will have authority over every tribe, tongue, and nation.

THE SAME TEST

Every person who will not withstand the persecution of the Antichrist and this final test for the body of Christ will turn from worshiping Jesus to worshiping the Antichrist. Just like it is today, our worship will indicate our hearts in the last days. Only a person who knows Him can truly worship Jesus and is, therefore, a person that is born again.

"But the hour is coming, and now is, when the true worshipers will worship the Father in spirit and truth; for the Father is seeking such to worship Him" (John 4:23, NKJV).

Our worship will decide where we will spend eternity. In the last days, the worship of the Father will intensify, and so will the worship of the devil.

"So they worshiped the dragon who gave authority to the beast; and they worshiped the beast, saying, 'Who is like the beast? Who is able to make war with him?'" (Revelation 13:4, NKJV).

John's vision tells us that every single person who is not written in the Book of Life, every person who will not worship the Father in spirit and in truth, will worship the devil.

"All who dwell on the earth will worship him, whose names have not been written in the Book of Life of the Lamb slain from the foundation of the world" (Revelation 13:8, NKJV).

ENDURING THE SWORD

In verse 9, John suddenly pauses the recalling of his vision by saying, "If anyone has an ear, let him hear" (Revelation 13:9, NKJV).

It is interesting that John would pause recalling his vision with these eight words. While it is a short statement, I believe it is of utmost importance. I believe that what John reiterates to the reader of the vision is how important it is to listen with our spiritual ears and not our natural ears. People who hear this vision with their natural ears might reject the severity and the truth of this vision. John is ensuring that whoever reads his vision understands that he received it from God, that it is for the church, and that the church must grasp the importance of this vision. I believe that John had a sense that many Christians would perhaps reject this real and challenging vision of the end times. He challenges all of us to have an ear for what God is saying, to not run away from revelation truth, but to receive it with an open heart and mind.

So, "If anyone has an ear, let him hear" (Revelation 13:9, NKJV).

John then continues to share the vision that he received:

"He who leads into captivity shall go into captivity; he who kills with the sword must be killed with the sword. Here is the patience and the faith of the saints" (Revelation 13:10, NKJV).

This verse once again speaks about the persecution that will come upon the Christians. The wave of persecution that will be unleashed will truly test the patience and the faith of all believers, but those who are patient to endure and those who have faith to not give up will prevail for eternity. Patience is a huge part of faith. To wait patiently for God to fulfill His promises in our lives is a strong statement of faith. The impatient are the ones who lack faith. For the global church to patiently endure the persecution that is to come will be a powerful declaration of faith. It will be the trademark of the spotless bride as she will be patiently waiting for her Bridegroom to come.

INTENSIFIED DECEPTION

> Then I saw another beast coming up out of the earth, and he had two horns like a lamb and spoke like a dragon. And he exercises all the authority of the first beast in his presence, and causes the earth and those who dwell in it to worship the first beast, whose deadly wound was healed. He performs great signs, so that he even makes fire come down from heaven on the earth in the sight of men. And he deceives those who dwell on the earth by those signs which he was granted to do in the sight of the beast, telling those who dwell on the earth to make an image to the beast who was wounded by the sword and lived. He was granted power to give breath to the image of the beast, that the image of the beast should both speak and cause as many as would not worship the image of the beast to be killed. He causes all, both small and great, rich and poor, free and slave, to receive a mark on their right hand or on their foreheads, and that no one may buy or sell except one who has the mark or the name of the beast, or the number of his name.
>
> Revelation 13:11–17 (NKJV)

The rest of John's vision gives us new details about another person who will rise to power and aid the Antichrist in his mission. This person is called by many "the false prophet." His mission will be to intensify the Antichrist's deception upon earth with lying signs and wonders. All those who are easily moved by the supernatural will quickly fall for this false prophet, as he will perform mighty signs and wonders. All those who are at that time not living in the written Word of God on a continuous basis will be deceived by this prophet.

Just like today, in those days, the truth of scripture and close communion with the Spirit of truth, the Holy Spirit, will be the only lifeline. The devil has power, and he is able to perform mighty miracles, but his signs and wonders will always lack truth. His miracles will always lack the truth that only Jesus is the way, the truth, and the life and that only Jesus deserves all honor, glory, and worship.

This false prophet will call for people to worship the Antichrist on the streets and in their homes. Anyone who will not worship the Antichrist will be killed, and anyone who will not engrave his sign on their hand or forehead will not be allowed to sell or buy. These actions will, once again, test the body of Christ. There will be Christian farmers with full grain silos who won't be able to sell their grain. There will be Christian farmers who won't be able to buy the fuel needed to harvest the fields. There will be Christian mothers who won't be able to buy food for their kids. There will be sick Christians who will be refused service. There will be Christian realtors unable to sell or buy homes, or there will be Christian carpenters not able to sell their services. Not being able to buy or sell will eventually cause poverty and hunger.

How will the body react when faced with poverty and hunger? Will people give up, or will people patiently endure? Will their faith be quenched or their faith activated? Will they, in faith, receive miraculous provisions from their ever-caring heavenly Father, or will they, lacking faith, open their hands to the government of the Antichrist? Will Christians work together and love their neighbors more than themselves, or will they turn to greed and withholding? Will the bride unite under these pressures of hunger and poverty? Will the bride unify and get herself ready for the coming of the bridegroom? Will denominational borders fall, and Christ's love prevail among us? Those are all questions that will be answered in those days. God's love will not fail, nor will His grace fail; His heart will be for all of us to endure and overcome.

According to John's vision, the end-time church will face all these trials. I felt it was important to give you an insight into John's vision in light of sharing the meaning of Daniel's vision with you. My heart is not to discourage anyone, nor do I want to cause fear in anyone's heart. I wrote all of this because it is of utmost importance that the church faces these things that will come and that we prepare our hearts and minds. This preparation cannot be delayed any longer, but it must begin today. While it is not bad to make earthly provisions for the days ahead, I believe the emphasis must be on making spiritual provisions. Walk in love instead of fear today. Walk in closeness with God today. Search your heart today and make a commitment to Christ today, so when the trials begin, you are already dwelling in the shadow of the Almighty.

— CHAPTER 17: —
YOUR TURN TO RESPOND

In this book, I have given many insights into Daniel's end-time vision, John's end-time vision, and the current state of the church. Now, it is your turn to respond.

If this book has touched your heart and if you believe that what was shared was a revelation truth, the worst thing you can do is to do nothing. God will use scripture, people, dreams, visions, sermons, prophecies, and many other things to get our attention. Whenever He gets our attention, whenever He stirs our heart, whenever He convicts us, and whenever He speaks to us, it is very important that we not only receive from Him but that we *respond* to Him. "To respond" means "to act and to put actions toward what stirs us deep inside." If we delay our response, often, the fire that God sparked within us will die, and His stirring will become dormant again.

I encourage you to respond right now to what you read in this. Open your eyes and keep them open. Open your ears and keep them open. Go and act according to what is happening right before your eyes. Do not get pulled into conspiracy theories, but judge the times with the help of the Holy Spirit and the written Word. Do not just focus on all the bad that is happening without building His kingdom. Let urgency and love stir your heart through the power of the Holy Spirit to build God's kingdom while it is still light.

This is not the end and every new day is another day to preach Jesus, to revive and reform the church, to be a godly parent and a loving neighbor. Invest more time into your kids and prepare them to be steadfast in the face of what is coming. Pray that they would fall head over heels in love with Jesus. Strengthen the church, commit to your local church so that it will become a true haven for lost souls. Carry the burdens of fellow Christians who are overwhelmed and beaten up by the spirit of this age. Teach truth, preach truth, and pray for the leaders of your nation to return to God. Do not give up and do not give in, for God is faithful, and He loves you.

I would like to end this book with a prayer. If you agree with this prayer, feel free to pray it as well:

> Father, I pray that you would speak to every person who has read this book. Father, I pray that you would open our eyes and our ears to what your Spirit is speaking in this hour. Open our eyes to see what is happening in this world and give us the love and the courage to respond. Open our understanding and give us revelation truth in this dry and barren land. Fill us with your Holy Spirit and grant us to be used for your kingdom. Father, we will not be afraid of the increasing darkness. Father, we will not run from the truth. Father, we will not give up but we will stand firmly on your Son Jesus Christ. Father let us experience the pure and passionate love of your Son Jesus. Let us be engulfed with His love and let us bring it to those who are lost. In all of our ways we acknowledge your goodness, your love and your everlasting care. No matter what our eyes will see, we commit ourselves to you and choose to trust you. In Jesus' name, we pray. Amen!

– ABOUT THE AUTHOR –

Jonathan Frohms is an apostolic voice, teacher, author, and revivalist. His heart beats for the body of Christ to come to its full potential and destiny. After several years on the mission field in Africa, God called him to America with the mission to revive the church. The Lord spoke to him and said, *"Go to America and preach the Gospel, for my people are confused."* With this mandate and a deep love for the United States, Jonathan and his family moved to America. He and his wife, Mary, and their four children live in North Dakota, where he currently pastors Harvest Church. He is also leading an apostolic ministry that focuses on building up and equipping churches all over the United States, Central America, and beyond.